Warrior Princess Of God

Book 2 (May - Aug)

Sarah B. Odom, PhD

Contributing Editor - Mel Ann Sullivan

In Memory

This devotional book is written in loving memory of **Marjorie L. Lauderdale**. Marjorie was a vivacious, independent woman who was definitely a picture of class, charm, and wit. Just as the women in this devotional book have stories and their own unique personalities, Marjorie was definitely one of a kind. It was an honor to be a small insignificant part of her life, and she probably never knew the true impact she had on mine. I will miss her. As a young girl, I sure loved her high heels. Her smile was infectious, and she did not mind telling you what she thought. We need more authentic women in this world today. She wasn't perfect, but she was a perfect warrior princess.

Contents

Acknowledgements

This book is inspired by the many women who have struggles and stories containing colorful pasts, deep sorrow, a need to restart, and the desire to be heard. While we all have the potential to be a warrior princess, not everyone was born in the palace. Many of us fight our way into the royal family every day. Many of us struggle and have difficulties that are almost unbearable. It is for those of us who struggle most, I write this book.

It matters not whether you most identify with Rahab, Miriam, Ruth, or Hannah, you will most certainly find something within each of these women that will help you in your spiritual journey in life. These women have powerful stories to share with us, and even though centuries separate our lives, we still have much to learn.

If you find yourself thinking, "I don't have anything in common with this woman or that woman," I ask you to just STOP. No one is watching you other than God, and He knows already. We all have like passions; we all have struggles with sin, lust, and temptations. If you will take the opportunity to see how these women prevailed, perhaps you will find strength for today's battle or for tomorrow's warfare. It's a privilege to share the lives of these women through these pages and with you. May God richly bless you.

Introduction

Old Testament women have vibrant stories. Each one is special, and the ways in which God uses her life brings the story of our relationship with our Creator into perspective with each stroke of the pen. Out of all the thousands, even millions of women who lived throughout history, there must be some special reason God placed these specific stories in our paths. What will we learn from them?

So many times we have this idea in order to be a warrior princess, you must be perfect. Nothing could be further from the truth. God uses our imperfections to reveal His glory in our lives. He used a harlot to overthrow a wicked city. He used an older sister with jealousy issues to be a leader in Israel. God took a Moabite woman, whose tribe was often at war with the Israelites, and made her an ancestor of Christ. God also used a broken, barren woman to give birth to one of the greatest prophets to ever grace this planet.

Do not place your restraints on God; don't try to determine who can and cannot be used. He does incredible things in the lives of those He loves. The Bible tells us He loves all who will turn to Him. God can and will use your life, and He can and will use the lives of those who seem to be the most unworthy. Stand back, and stand amazed!

May
Rahab - The Negotiator

Scripture Reading - Verses relating to the story of Rahab as well as other verses on loyalty and being chosen.

Rahab was called a harlot (whore or adulterous woman; prostitute or promiscuous woman) by Biblical writers. Certainly those who wrote about her wanted us to understand her background. Yet amazingly even with her colorful past, she recognized how powerful God was. She wanted to be protected by a God like Him. Rahab risked everything to hide the Israelite spies sent to scout out Jericho. But somehow, in her pagan heart, she knew she would be just fine if she was so strongly compelled to hide them.

Your life's story may not be so colorful. Yet, I somehow feel we can learn much from Rahab. Her life was important to God. He inspired several Biblical authors record her history. Her purposeful placement in the lineage of Christ illuminates the character of God and His forgiveness. The greatest theme shining from Rahab's story is for us not to worry so much about our past or present, but to look to our future with God. Her story can help us build our confidence and trust God keeps His promises. God has no problems saving a person who wants to be saved!

DAY 1

Scripture Reading: Joshua 2: 1-5

Rahab's name comes from three Hebrew letters - reish, hei, and beit. When you look at the meaning of each letter, something amazing jumps out of the ancient text. *Reish* means "beginning". *Hei* usually symbolizes a "window," and *beit* always means "house." There are multiple ways we can draw analogies, like Rahab was the beginning of a window for Israel to conquer Jericho. Or, Rahab was the beginning of a window into the House of David. It's true; she was a significant character in the events leading to final entry into the Promised Land.

Pondering Thoughts:

Do you wonder if Rahab ever dreamed she would be such an integral part of the lineage of David, and more importantly of the lineage of Christ? Do you ever stop and ask yourself, "What is planned for my life?" Or, "Am I a door for something spectacular in the future?" Perhaps we don't think enough about our importance to God despite our own shortcomings. As true as it was for Rahab, it's true for you and me. We are the handiwork of God who set us apart before the foundation of the world to do good works prepared in advance for us (Ephesians 2:10).

Praise and Petitions:

Chief Cornerstone, I know you are certainly the beginning of all things. Without you nothing would exist. I praise your Holiness and thank you for putting your Spirit into my life. Help me to understand and realize the importance of my life to you and your plan. I ask this in your name, Amen.

Prayer Journaling Notes:

Points from the Editor:

One thing we often discount is the value of one life in a family line. One life that will be the end of alcoholism... The beginning of a college educated generation... The beginning of living with integrity... The end of poverty... The first homeowner or the first financially fit... And best of all - the first true lover of Jesus. Rahab was the one. You can be too.

Questions and Reflections:

1. What stood out to you in the scripture reading today?

2. Answer at least one of the pondering questions?

3. Personalize the prayer for your own life below:

DAY 2

Scripture Reading: Joshua 2: 6-10

Rahab's name has several meanings associated with it. Some of them are pagan and harsh, such as insolence, fierceness, savage, and hostile. But others are more generous, like roomy and "at liberty." Rahab did not have control over what she was named, but she could affect the outcome how her name would be remembered. Very few people actually take the time and legal steps to change their names in life, but we can work daily toward how we will be remembered.

Pondering Thoughts:

What do people think when they hear your given name? How have I lived in this life that would harm my name, and how have I lived that would give credit to my name? How would you answer these questions? How have those answers changed with time and maturity?

Praise and Petitions:

Deliverer, I praise you for your ability to take a broken life and completely remake it into your image. You truly bring beauty from ashes. Help me to protect those things you have given me, especially when my name is associated with your name. Help me to represent the Kingdom well. I ask this in your name, Amen.

Prayer Journaling Notes:

Points from the Editor:

Even as a Christian from a very young age, I didn't think about my legacy. I thought an awful lot about what I wanted in life for me. We do live in such a selfish, entertainment seeking society. God used babies (it took three) to show me I would only leave behind that which I possess. My life would be the kickstart for their futures. At that moment, God showed me my life mattered for generations to come in the same way the lives of my own parents mattered for mine.

Questions and Reflections:

1. What stood out to you in the scripture reading today?

2. Answer at least one of the pondering questions?

3. Personalize the prayer for your own life below:

DAY 3

Scripture Reading: Joshua 2:11-15

Several scriptural references in the Old and New Testament speak of Rahab as living the life of a harlot prior to her encounter with the Israelites. There's no doubt, from Christian standards, Rahab had a very promiscuous past. Perhaps many of us would not have even gone into her home if our lives had depended on it. But the spies, one of which may have been Salmon (her future husband), took a chance on her. They went to see her for help. They saw worth in Rahab, obviously for what they could gain. They trusted her with their very lives. Rahab saw her own worth, and she made a pact to save herself and her family. Even colorful people are worthy to God and worth saving.

Pondering Thoughts:

Are you a person with a questionable past? How does the fact God so loves you penetrate deeply into your heart? How do you treat people you know who have a questionable past or present? Based on God's example of Rahab, how might you alter your approach?

Praise and Petitions:

Gracious and Merciful God, I am thankful you have forgiven me for my past. I also thank you for giving me a future in your Kingdom. I ask you to help me realize the worth of all mankind and to look beyond what a person may have been or is today. Help me see the promise of the future. I ask this in your name, Amen.

Prayer Journaling Notes:

Points from the Editor:

As seasoned believers, we often forget what our lives were like when we were not in love with Jesus. We forget for good reason, because Christ forgets also as He hurls our sins as far as the east is from the west. He remembers them no more. But we must never forget what forgiveness looks like on our lives. Judgment is a terrible thing, something the perfect Son of God experienced six different times in less than 48 or so hours by leaders and sects trying to wrongfully accuse Him. Then, He was nailed to the cross of His temporary death. He was perfect. We all deserved death, but He took it for us. James tells us mercy always triumphs over judgment. Paul tells us it is loving kindness that draws someone to repentance. This, my friend, is the charge of love God has given us for one another.

Questions and Reflections:

1. What stood out to you in the scripture reading today?

2. Answer at least one of the pondering questions?

3. Personalize the prayer for your own life below:

DAY 4

Scripture Reading: Joshua 2:16-20

I have often wondered what Rahab saw in the spies of Israel that caused Rahab to risk with her life and the lives of her family. Had she been caught, she would have likely been treated like a person who had committed treason. But something allowed her faith in the God of the Israelites to outweigh her fear of being caught. Opening our hearts to God's messengers (or spies in this event) may seem a little risky. We may even doubt the intent of those who come in the name of the Lord. But there comes a time in our lives when we humbly trust God, even if it's risky.

Pondering Thoughts:

So, what would you have done if two spies had come to your house? What if someone needed you to keep a dangerous or threatening secret? How would you do it? What would be your response to taking a risky action for God?

Praise and Petitions:

Immanuel, I praise you for your willingness to take a risk on humanity. Given our track record, it is truly amazing you did. I ask for your guidance and help when you send someone my way in whom you would like for me to take a risk. It's not always easy for me to trust someone. I tend to shy away for a while, or I wind up trusting someone I shouldn't have. I need discernment. I ask this in your name, Amen.

Prayer Journaling Notes:

Points from the Editor:

In at least one Biblical definition of the word "discern," the meaning of judgment was never noted. But the following statements may help us to frame up in our minds the best ways to discern before taking risks. When we discern in advance, we actually are calculating risks before taking them:

- *When faced with a potentially risky venture, I will scrutinize or look intently at the situation before making a move.*
- *I will acknowledge the situation before God, and disclose my thoughts or questions.*
- *I will become well acquainted with every angle of possible risk, asking such questions as "What do I have to lose?" "Do I have something to gain.?" and "What interest or business is this of mine?"*
- *When I have my suspicions or even reservations, I will, however respectfully, disregard, ignore, reject the risk, and distance myself.*

Questions and Reflections:

1. What stood out to you in the scripture reading today?

2. Answer at least one of the pondering questions?

3. Personalize the prayer for your own life below:

DAY 5

Scripture Reading: Joshua 2: 21-24

Opening up such a vulnerable part of your life to an outsider is not easy. I tend to hold back and watch carefully for a while before I will let someone unfamiliar come into my life. Then there have been times in my life where I have opened up, and later I wished I hadn't. I am almost certain Rahab was worried she might be double-crossed, and yet somehow she had the courage to go ahead with the risk. I truly admire her for this trait, and perhaps I am just a little envious of her.

Pondering Thoughts:

How vulnerable are you when it comes to opening up to others? When faced with a situation in which you must trust someone you really don't know, how do you respond? How do you vet those in whom you put your confidence?

Praise and Petitions:

King of Glory, thank you for understanding we are vulnerable without your help. I stand amazed at how you have protected me and my family through the years when I didn't vet some people as much as I should have. I also thank you for allowing me to open my heart to those you wanted in my life. Help me to become trusting when I need to trust and to be cautious when your Spirit restrains me. I ask this in your name, Amen.

Prayer Journaling Notes:

Points from the Editor:

It seems the older I get, the less I trust others and the more I trust God. I'm not there yet, though. In God's Word we are often admonished to be wise, not ignorant of the ways of man and the ruler of this world. We hear an awful lot today about vetting of immigrants, of contracts and business relationships. We should do more of it for our own lives without becoming a barricade that blocks out all things God wants on the inside. When you vet out a matter, you are wise. You carefully examine with a skillful and critical eye. You seek to verify the accuracy of the data, the authenticity of the source, and the validity of the concern or issue. That takes some time. The process of vetting flies in the face of the impatient soul and the one who likes to take action and move on. Vetting is worth the wait.

Questions and Reflections:

1. What stood out to you in the scripture reading today?

2. Answer at least one of the pondering questions?

3. Personalize the prayer for your own life below:

DAY 6

Scripture Reading: Joshua 3: 1-5

Rahab hid the Israelite spies in her flax on the roof of her home. In other words, she hid them in plain site, yet they were well hidden. The men from Jericho obviously did not take the time to look for the spies in her workroom; they seemingly only looked for them in her bedroom. They made a critical error in judgment of Rahab, and as a result it cost them finding the spies and ultimately their city and their lives. This should warn us of making judgment calls on people who are complicated to say the least.

Pondering Thoughts:

What was it about the flax that caused the men of Jericho to disregard it although it was an excellent hiding place? Do you ever disregard someone's value because of a past he/she may have? If so, how should you really evaluate a person? The next time God places a person in your path that makes you feel uneasy or embarrassed, how will you respond?

Praise and Petitions:

Jesus Christ the Righteous, you truly are the only righteous One, yet so many times we often feel we are. I am amazed at your patience towards humanity. Thank you for giving us multiple opportunities to get things right. Help me to see what you want me to see in others. Don't let me miss something crucial because I can't see past something colorful in a person's life. I ask this in your name, Amen.

Prayer Journaling Notes:

Points from the Editor:

My oldest brother is mentally ill - severe paranoia schizophrenia. Growing up with him was wonderful until he was in his early adult years. He was my vigilante, defending me against a then more jealous brother. He could quickly put a stop to bullying! But once his mental disorder became apparent, I was embarrassed and uneasy around him. However, God used my relationship with this brother to teach me so much about love, forgiveness, life, and true mental illness. We often underestimate the wholistic view of a person God created. Their sins are common to man. Their errors in judgment are more like our own than we want to admit. God will bring people into our lives to push our buttons, to bring out of us what He wants to be removed from our lives. Our response is key, and prayer is the priority.

Questions and Reflections:

1. What stood out to you in the scripture reading today?

2. Answer at least one of the pondering questions?

3. Personalize the prayer for your own life below:

DAY 7

Scripture Reading: Joshua 3: 6-10

Of the many talents Rahab had, she was a great protector and diverter. The men in Jericho never suspected Rahab of harboring the spies once they visited her home. She got the men from Jericho out of her home and on the wrong path very quickly. That is a tactical and strategic thinker. She knew how to protect those whom God wanted protected. We can take her example and be better equipped at leading the enemy away from our loved ones. This is warfare, and we need to be shrewd.

Pondering Thoughts:

How well do you plan your tactical battles in spiritual warfare? How has the enemy come into your home or church in the past year? How did you help to combat this attack or infiltration? What are some ways you will divert his attention in the future?

Praise and Petitions:

Majesty on High, I love you, and I praise you for helping your children. You provide guidance and support while we are in the battle for our souls. When we turn towards you, you help us prevail in ways that are unimaginable. Help me to lean on you and move in the direction of your Spirit as I battle my enemy. I ask this in your name, Amen.

Prayer Journaling Notes:

Points from the Editor:

I had seen the head-to-toe prayer for your husband a number of times. I had actually prayed some of these scriptures over his life throughout the years. But recently it became clear to me God wanted me to use this prayer pattern every day in my morning quiet time. Within just weeks, I understood why. When God compels you to set up barricades, to prepare for warfare, to guard your mind, and to listen intently, do it. He knows what is ahead. He is preparing you for war, sleepless nights, and times of great struggle. He is strengthening you for battles you cannot even fathom. This life we live in Christ is pounded out in a fallen world marked by Satan's reign. God has given us the weapons of warfare - the same ones He used in the ultimate battle for our souls. But the duty falls to the soldier to pick them up, even if trembling with fear, and use them.

Questions and Reflections:

1. What stood out to you in the scripture reading today?

2. Answer at least one of the pondering questions?

3. Personalize the prayer for your own life below:

DAY 8

Scripture Reading: Joshua 3: 11-17

Rahab told the spies she had heard of the God of the Israelites. The very mention of His name had brought terror among her people. They were not used to gods doing the kinds of things this God did. Rahab knew in her heart this was different. No one can compare to the Great God Jehovah. The mention of His name brings fear to those seeking for answers in life. Yet it seems the children often forget He is their Father. Sometimes it takes those who do not fully commit to Christ to remind us of the sacrifice He paid for us. This should not be.

Pondering Thoughts:

Do others revere and fear God more than you? How do you show your reverence for God? What kinds of actions do you display that would cause others to want to know more about God? These tough questions deserve honest answers.

Praise and Petitions:

Only Begotten Son of God, I praise your name. You are known throughout the world and feared by those who recognize your power. Help me to stay focused on your power as well as your loving kindness. Help me to relay your majesty to others. I ask this in your name, Amen.

Prayer Journaling Notes:

Points from the Editor:

When we come to know God through intimacy of relationship, the fear is different. The fear is reverent; I've come to the place in my life I am not scared of what will happen if I obey Him. I wouldn't want the consequences of not obeying Him. It's a huge flip in the spiritual life of a child of God. To not act when God has clearly spoken does not hid the fact He did speak - God Himself! We can pretend we didn't hear Him, presume we didn't completely understand, or procrastinate because we aren't sure where to start. But all He wanted and requires is obedience. If He required it of His own Son, He will require it of us. It's quite liberating to walk through a door He alone has opened and do what He alone has asked of you. That's up to us, but the rest is up to Him.

Questions and Reflections:

1. What stood out to you in the scripture reading today?

2. Answer at least one of the pondering questions?

3. Personalize the prayer for your own life below:

DAY 9

Scripture Reading: Joshua 4: 1-5

Rahab speaks of the inhabitants of the land melting and losing courage at the mention of the God of Israel. She recognized He was the only God who could save her. Though her name is derived from the Egyptian god, Ra, she knew only this God - the God of Israel - could save her and her family from His wrath. She did not trust in Ra or any other pagan god which may have existed in Jericho. She placed her trust in God, El, I Am, Yahweh. This speaks volumes for her faith in the unseen God. She chose sides that day. The choice is free to all men. It is the gift of God called free will, gifted to mankind. Many will choose righteously; others will choose damnation to their souls.

Pondering Thoughts:

There is a song that begs the question, "Which way will you choose?" That is a very powerful question. What do you choose this day? Which direction will you take when it matters most?

Praise and Petitions:

Redeemer, I thank you for the redemption of Israel, and I certainly thank you for the redemption of the Gentiles. I thank you for the grace you have extended to me. Help me never take this grace for granted. Empower me to lead others to you while this grace still exists. I ask this in your name, Amen.

Prayer Journaling Notes:

Points from the Editor:

God is sovereign. When our will doesn't align with His, free will is the gift. It's the gift that allows us the liberty to do life independently from God. It's the gift that, when accompanied by the indwelling of the Spirit of God, allows us the complete privilege of doing life in total dependence on Him. Obedience is rewarded. We may not see how in this life, but we will eventually meet eyes with our very great reward. Until then, the road is bumpy at times, smooth in some parts, and hard to traverse in other places. But the One who first walked it knows what lies ahead and has experienced far worse and far more than we ever will. And for the joy set before Him, He endured the cross. He did that for me. He did that for you, my friend. Let that settle on your fears and transform your faith forever.

Questions and Reflections:

1. What stood out to you in the scripture reading today?

2. Answer at least one of the pondering questions?

3. Personalize the prayer for your own life below:

DAY 10

Scripture Reading: Joshua 4: 6-10

In a land of hostile people, the spies found favor with Rahab, and she showed them kindness. Kindness is such a powerful character trait. God speaks much of kindness throughout the scriptures, yet we live in a world that can be very harsh and cruel. So many times it seems like we have become a people who are angry and want revenge. We close up our bowels of mercy, and we seemingly have forgotten the place from where Jesus has pulled our souls. God still honors kindness just like He did for Rahab. Because of her kindness to two men, God saved her entire household and all their possessions. That is the power of kindness!

Pondering Thoughts:

If you were asked to rate your kindness on a scale from 1-10, where would you place yourself? Do you find it easier to be kind to family or strangers? Why? If your family were asked to honestly rate you for kindness, how would they rate your kindness towards them? towards others?

Praise and Petitions:

Strength of Israel, I praise you for your kindness. You are the ultimate example of what kindness should be. You extend your hand of friendship and mercy to anyone who wants to receive it. I ask you to help me be the kind person you would have me be. I ask these things in your name, Amen.

Prayer Journaling Notes:

Points from the Editor:

Sometimes it's hard to be kind. As He hung on the cross, Jesus asked His Father to show the kindness of forgiveness to His accusers, to the ones who pounded the nails into His flesh... the ones who mocked Him, spat on Him, whipped Him, and raised His mostly naked and wounded body on a cross into the sky. It's easy to show kindness to those who love you. Why wouldn't you? It's not impossible to show kindness in the face of hatred. The God who empowers you to live in the light of His love is doing it through you. You don't have to show it. You just have to let Him show it through you. True and pure kindness is not motivated out of revenge or unforgiveness. If so, God did not show it through you. You showed it on your own, but not at all for His Glory. Let Him. You will be so blessed in the end.

Questions and Reflections:

1. What stood out to you in the scripture reading today?

2. Answer at least one of the pondering questions?

3. Personalize the prayer for your own life below:

DAY 11

Scripture Reading: Joshua 4: 11-15

Rahab requested kindness in return from the spies she protected. She had something very valuable to her - her family. She begged for the safety of her father, mother, sister, brothers, and all they had. She also asked for her own life. Rahab knew the God of Israel was a just God. If she provided sanctuary to His spies, He would certainly return the kindness upon her and her family. Rahab cared for her family when it counted most. She loved their lives, and she would do anything to secure their safety. Her love extended further than her siblings, but to anyone associated with them. She was a great daughter, sister, and aunt. Though her life may have been colorful, there's no doubt where her loyalties lay. She loved her family.

Pondering Thoughts:

Family matters most. How far would you go to save the lives of your family members? What brings your family close? What are some things that cause distance between you and family members? How will you close that gap (if one exists) between you and your family members? What is your plan for restoration if one is needed? Do it today!

Praise and Petitions:

Consuming Fire, I thank you for your salvation. I pray for my family and their safety daily. I love my family, and I don't want to have anything in my heart or life that would cause a wedge or distance to form. Help me be the daughter, sibling, wife, mother, grandmother, mother-in-law, aunt, cousin, or other familial connection you would have me be. I ask this in your name, Amen.

Prayer Journaling Notes:

Points from the Editor:

Family - the ones worth fighting for... it's part of the legacy God has placed inside of me. Until one of the most troubling times in my family years ago, I had no idea I had a fight like that inside of me. Really, I didn't. I was full of fear. I should have been on medication. It was like that for me. Have you ever been there? But something deep down to my core said, "Girl, this family is God's gift to you." That voice inside of me was the start of my fight for what was mine. Satan had no territory here, not on that day, not ever. I stood up to him in the power of the name and blood of Jesus. He messed with the wrong child, the wrong family. Not ever would I go down, and I would be fighting from my knees, flat on my back, driving down the road, flat on my face... whenever... wherever... Every moment. Sister, a mighty warrior princess makes the enemy sorry he ever messed with you. You are that warrior. She's in there - by the power of the blood and name of the Mighty One.

Questions and Reflections:

1. What stood out to you in the scripture reading today?

2. Answer at least one of the pondering questions?

3. Personalize the prayer for your own life below:

DAY 12

Scripture Reading: Joshua 4: 16-20

Rahab asked the spies for a symbol, but not just any token, she wanted a "true token." She wanted assurance she would be protected. One of the things I love about God is the signs He gives us. God cares enough about His people He doesn't mind sending us a pledge of assurance when we need it most. The greatest demonstration He gave of His love was His Only Begotten Son - Jesus. Knowing Rahab asked for a token gives me courage to ask for signs from God. I want to know if I'm doing the right thing. I want to know my family will be saved. So, like Rahab, I seek God for signs and tokens in life that give me peace and understanding He has everything under control.

Pondering Thoughts:

What kinds of signs have you received from God in your past? How do you look for signs from God? What is something you seek from God currently in your life or in the lives of those you love? How will you know if God has sent you an answer?

Praise and Petitions:

Great Shepherd of the Sheep, I thank you for the marvelous signs and wonders you send throughout the earth. And I particularly thank you for the personal signs and tokens of love you send my way. Help me to seek you for signs, for I know your Word tells me to seek in order to find. Help me to show your signs to others so they may believe and be saved. I ask this in you name, Amen.

Prayer Journaling Notes:

Points from the Editor:

A token is often discounted by everyone you try to explain it to when God has provided it. But you know it. It's often an immediate knowing. God has His way of piercing our hearts for the purpose of confirming His word to us, even when we have not asked for a sign. God knows what we need even if it's not on our tongue or in our prayers. He gives us that sign when He knows we need it to move ahead in faith. He's good that way. He is that intimate. What good father does not give his children what they need? A word of caution - don't look for signs and tokens outside the word of God if you are not looking for them inside of it. He gave us His Word - this sign of His love and plan will never fade. It will never be snuffed out.

Questions and Reflections:

1. What stood out to you in the scripture reading today?

2. Answer at least one of the pondering questions?

3. Personalize the prayer for your own life below:

DAY 13

Scripture Reading: Joshua 4: 21-24

Rahab was given a promise. The men promised her she would be saved if she did not utter a word about the business they had done with her and in Jericho. She gave her word. They gave their word. That seemed to be enough for all of them. No long laborious contracts. No lawyers required. Just the power of the word. We should strive to have the same kind of power simply by giving our word in a world where it has come to mean so little. There is much power in the word - the power of life and death. It defines who we are: someone who can be trusted, or not.

Pondering Thoughts:

What do you look for in a person who gives his/her word? How would you be rated by others on the power of your own word? What steps do you take to ensure you keep your word once it is given?

Praise and Petitions:

Judge of all the Earth, I know you spoke all things into existence by the power of your word. I understand you give great emphasis in the scriptures on the power of a person's word. Help me to be honest and trustworthy. Help me do what is right so I do not reflect poorly on my word or your Word. I ask this in your name, Amen.

Prayer Journaling Notes:

Points from the Editor:

I say too much. I talk to much! Silence kills me! In a room full of people, I feel a tugging inside - a tugging to make everyone feel comfortable, to feel at home - even if it's not my own, for goodness sake! I want my words to mean something, don't you? I'd rather follow the leadership of the Spirit, the gentle nudge to quiet my own soul. I'm better at understanding the compelling to speak truth. But to be quiet, that's harder. What will people think? Will they think I'm angry? Or unwilling? Or uncomfortable? I want to be careful with my words in the wake of suffering. I want to be guarded, putting a muzzle over my mouth in the presence of the unfamiliar. God spoke, and things not yet created sprang to life. I want my words to birth something for His glory, and to kill something intended for evil. Self-control is the key.

Questions and Reflections:

1. What stood out to you in the scripture reading today?

2. Answer at least one of the pondering questions?

3. Personalize the prayer for your own life below:

DAY 14

Scripture Reading: Joshua 5: 1-5

Rahab used a cord to allow the spies to flee. This was an act of trust on their part, and an act of trustworthiness on her part. The Bible tells us her house was in the wall of the city, or town. She carefully allowed the spies to leave Jericho through her window, and they had to trust her completely with their lives. She could have yelled for the men of Jericho to capture them, and she would have likely been hailed a great warrior for her people. She could have dropped them to their death with the cord, and no one would likely know what happened to them. Yet, Rahab chose to use their vulnerability to prove to them she could be trusted. When it counted most, she came through for them.

Pondering Thoughts:

How easily do others trust you? How easily do you trust others? Where do you hold back from trusting in your life? Where do you hold back from completely trusting God? What are some things you can do to improve your trustworthiness as well as your ability to trust?

Praise and Petitions:

My High Tower, I praise you for your watchful care over me and my family. Thank you for always being the tower of safety we need. You are the most awesome refuge. Help me to point others to the refuge they can find in you. I want to be able to lead others to safety. I ask this in your name, Amen.

Prayer Journaling Notes:

Points from the Editor:

Trustworthiness - It's one of my core values. I want to be trusted with a dollar or a million, a secret or a strategy. This is what trust looks like to me based on Biblical truth:

> *Lord, to be trustworthy is to be dependable, blameless, a confidant, and stable and firm. To be too trusting is dangerous, and it can lead to wrong assumptions about others.*
> *Lord I know a difficulty of trusting others at all can lead to a lack of transparency, honesty, and hindered relationships long-term.*
> *I know it is balance that is needed. A completely radical trust in you alone is the way to this balance. I count on you to help me discern when and how I can trust. I lean on you to help me be trustworthy in every way.*

Questions and Reflections:

1. What stood out to you in the scripture reading today?

2. Answer at least one of the pondering questions?

3. Personalize the prayer for your own life below:

DAY 15

Scripture Reading: Joshua 5: 6-10

Rahab had key access into and out of the city from the wall. She had the optimum position to see what might be coming for the city, or to escape from the city if necessary. Rahab was smart to have such a home. She had been careful in planning for the things life may send her way. Because of her planning she was in the ideal position to help God's spies. We need to position ourselves in life so we can help others. Not everyone has the talent or resources to be keepers of the wall. But if we do, we need to step up for the Kingdom.

Pondering Thoughts:

What resources or talents do you have in your life that would make you a keeper of the wall? Can you think of a time when God used you to make a difference in someone's life? Remind yourself of this time and journal how it made you feel to be used to protect or help someone else.

Praise and Petitions:

The Eternal God, thank you for every resource and talent you have provided in my life. I do not deserve your gifts, but I sincerely appreciate them. Help me to see the needs of others should you allow me to sit on the wall. I want to be an asset to the Kingdom, but I cannot do it without your blessing and provisions. I ask this in your name, Amen.

Prayer Journaling Notes:

Points from the Editor:

You've been the one who needed that person to stand on the wall for you. You've been the other person too - the one who sure was depended on for support. We, at one time or another, will be called upon to defend a wall... stand up for a friend or family members... or just simply be silently present in time of trouble. And it will mean the world to someone. It will result in treasure stored up in heaven. It will never be forgotten, at least not by the One who matters most.

Questions and Reflections:

1. What stood out to you in the scripture reading today?

2. Answer at least one of the pondering questions?

3. Personalize the prayer for your own life below:

DAY 16

Scripture Reading: Joshua 5: 11-15

Rahab was instructed to leave the same scarlet cord in her window when she knew the Israelites were about to strike. This cord became her lifeline. Even though the Israelite spies promised Rahab protection, it was contingent upon her actions. She had to keep quiet, and she had to place the scarlet cord in her window. There are so many times we ask for God's protection or His provision, but often God gives us instructions on what we need to do to make that happen. While we are not saved or lost based on our works, we do have to take action when God tells us to do so in order to see things happen in our lives and in the lives of our loved ones. Faith without works is dead.

Pondering Thoughts:

How will you respond to the call or the instructions God leaves for you to see the next movement you want to see? Do you have unsaved loved ones? What are you willing to do that they might see the light of Jesus and be drawn to salvation?

Praise and Petitions:

The True Vine, I thank you each day for your grafting in of my soul into the Kingdom. I am thankful I can be a true heir with Christ. Help me to do my part each and every day to build the Kingdom and win the lost at any cost. I ask this in your name, Amen.

Prayer Journaling Notes:

Points from the Editor:

Our preparation paves the way for God's protection. Prayers offered over the crib of a newborn baby remain active for the teen years, the freshman year of college, and the rebellious seasons. Time studying God's Word allows the planting of it inside the heart of His child who will later need to recite it during the midnight hours to keep anxiety, depression, or fear at bay. You see, God promises to perfect (or bring to an end result) that which concerns us. He's even saving our tears. Prepare when the going is good. Then, when life takes a treacherous turn, your Savior will bring to remembrance all those preparations when you need them most. He is faithful.

Questions and Reflections:

1. What stood out to you in the scripture reading today?

2. Answer at least one of the pondering questions?

3. Personalize the prayer for your own life below:

DAY 17

Scripture Reading: Joshua 6: 1-5

When the time drew near, Rahab gathered her people into her home. This scene is much different from Lot and his family. Lot did not have the influence over his family to save all of them from Sodom and Gomorrah's judgment. Yet, Rahab's family was saved by her actions. This proves Rahab's family saw something in her, as well as her stories of the God of Israel, that made them want to be saved. She had influence over her people. If we are going to win our loved ones for the Kingdom, we must have influence. They must see something in our lives that makes them want to learn more. Our influence needs to never waver.

Pondering Thoughts:

If you had to ask your family to trust you today, what would be their response? What are some things you can do as a believer and as a family member to build trust with your family? Name someone who has been a role model for you, and tell why you trusted that person.

Praise and Petitions:

The Truth, I can always count on you. Your name is truth; your being is truth. All except you is untrustworthy. You are the only absolute truth. I thank you for being able to fully trust you. Help me to become more like you. Help me when I falter in truth and trust. I want others to be able to count on me. I ask this in your name, Amen.

Prayer Journaling Notes:

Points from the Editor:

Influence (or impact) is another one of my core values. It's important to me to be a positive influence in my circle. This is what that looks like to me from a Biblical perspective:

> *Lord, I know influence can be good or bad. I choose to be concerned the good outweigh the bad, and understand that "perfect" is an illusion. I want to be transparently influential and share out of my own experiences so others see the "real" me and Christ in me. I am positively impacting those in my circle of influence, starting at home. My life at home can be held up to the "impact" test. I have pure motives in influencing others - to further the Kingdom, mentor, and model as Christ would have me. I continue to boldly encourage our Sunday school class to know what matters most.*

Questions and Reflections:

1. What stood out to you in the scripture reading today?

2. Answer at least one of the pondering questions?

3. Personalize the prayer for your own life below:

DAY 18

Scripture Reading: Joshua 6: 6-10

When Joshua gave the order to invade Jericho, everything was to be destroyed, except Rahab and her family. Joshua honored the pact the spies had made with her, and he instructed his soldiers to find her by looking for the scarlet cord. They were to make sure no harm came to her. When God makes a covenant, you can count on it. Joshua knew Rahab was counting on him to keep the covenant she had made with the spies, and he did. Rahab and all her father's household was spared because of what she did for those two spies that day.

Pondering Thoughts:

What special covenant are you counting on God to keep with you through your walk with Him? If you could use one thing to symbolize the scarlet cord in your life, what would that be? What are you waiting on God to perform for you?

Praise and Petitions:

Wonderful, you are so wonderful. You do more for me in one single day than I could repay in a lifetime of service and worship. I am so blessed to be a part of this wonderful Kingdom and family. Help me to keep my covenant with you and use me to build the Kingdom each day. I ask this in your name, Amen.

Prayer Journaling Notes:

Points from the Editor:

It's a fearful thing to think I might not be able to keep a promise or covenant. I want to. I need to. I would love to. It's part of who I am, but it's not always who I portray. One time I promised to be the friend who never would walk away. The promise was made on the inside, never to that person. She had been hurt by so many I didn't want to be one more statistic in her mind - another friendship gone bad. But I couldn't be what she couldn't understand about friendship. It hurt me to the core to have to cease the diplomacy and apologies, the conversations and clarity, and just step away. Better, to me, to make a commitment within yourself than a vow to the whole world. The commitment within can be more lasting.

Questions and Reflections:

1. What stood out to you in the scripture reading today?

2. Answer at least one of the pondering questions?

3. Personalize the prayer for your own life below:

DAY 19

Scripture Reading: Joshua 6: 11-15

Each day as Israel marched around the walls of Jericho, I can only imagine the anxiousness in Rahab's heart. I wonder if she ever thought they might forsake her. Did she think her own city might find out what she had done to betray them? On the final day, as Joshua and all of Israel made their way around Jericho those seven times, with each repetitious march, did her heart pound more and more? Rahab knew this much - on this day either her salvation or her destruction would come. We, too, have an impending date with Christ. Depending on our covenant with Him, we will either have a day of eternal salvation or eternal damnation. Christ will certainly keep His word. How will we stand or bow before Christ - justified and covered by His blood or condemned because we failed to repent and accept His gift of salvation? The choice is truly ours.

Pondering Thoughts:

What are you doing to prepare for the day that is coming to all when Christ will judge? We are all going to be judged according to our lives we lived while we waited for our bridegroom. What message do you give to those around you to help them prepare? What is your scarlet cord for your people?

Praise and Petitions:

The Word, since the beginning you have been the Word. Nothing exists without your speaking it into existence. I praise you for the power of your Word. I ask for your leading as I live out my days that have been allotted to me on earth. I want to be ready when the rest of the world is in chaos. I know the choice is mine, but please protect me and help me make the right one. In your name I pray, Amen.

Prayer Journaling Notes:

Points from the Editor:

Anxiety, whether in Rahab's heart or mine, steals away the trust that can be there in its place. Anxiety is a thief. It robs us blind, leaves us hopeless, grips our minds, and dashes our dreams. If all of the energy it takes from our bodies were accomplishing some result, then it might be worth all we sacrifice for it. But it's a drag, a negative demonic tool from hell itself. It has no place in the life of a believer. It's like a train that has run off the track and is just a wreck quick in the making. It's the trumped up idea a bear is chasing you through the woods, and you are doomed. Only nothing of the sort is actually happening. It could not be further from the truth. Anxiety imagines every crazy possibility to make you crazy. It's a farce. It needs to stop. It has no power for life.

Questions and Reflections:

1. What stood out to you in the scripture reading today?

2. Answer at least one of the pondering questions?

3. Personalize the prayer for your own life below:

DAY 20

Scripture Reading: Joshua 6: 16-20

The Bible tells us from the very day of the destruction of Jericho, Rahab lived among the Israelites. She had made her choice. She would become one of the traveling caravan of Hebrews headed through the Promised Land. This was such a turning point for Rahab. We all have likely had or will have monumental turning points in our lives. Those will be defining moments for us. In those moments we have to accept the changes that come our way, or we lose heart and become embittered. Rahab chose to live with a foreign people if it meant she and her family would be saved.

Pondering Thoughts:

What defining moments have you experienced in your life? How did you transition into those moments? How has your life changed? What would you do differently if you could to prepare yourself for the changes?

Praise and Petitions:

Consolation of Israel, I thank you for the defining moments you have sent in my life. I am truly sorry for the complaining I have done, and will likely continue to do in the future. I wish I were different. But I know with your help and mercy I can do better. Help me be the person you desire for me to be. I ask this in your name, Amen.

Prayer Journaling Notes:

Points from the Editor:

Transitions are ordained by God. They are designed by Him to move us from where we are to where He wants us to be. The place of transition requires monumental trust - trust in what you thought you could do dissipates right before your eyes. As you struggle through the changes, God is using the sand you've been standing on to show you a firm foundation, a rock stronger than money, a home, possessions, profession, a marriage, your health, your family, and your idols. He strips you down to the base of life. What do you need? What can you live without? What can you really count on? When Jesus is all you have, you will find He is really all you need. He's there in your future. He's redeeming your past. He's holding you tightly in the here and now. He rocks your world, and you will never be quite the same again.

Questions and Reflections:

1. What stood out to you in the scripture reading today?

2. Answer at least one of the pondering questions?

3. Personalize the prayer for your own life below:

DAY 21

Scripture Reading: Joshua 6: 21-27

Rahab walked away from everything she knew in Jericho to follow after a strange people who had been wandering around in a desert for over forty years. One of the reasons she decided to make this choice was because of the magnificent things she had heard about the God of the Israelites. The stories had created a longing in her heart to be a part of such a great multitude of people who were blessed by God, fed by God, led by God, and protected by God. We should never stop telling the stories about what God has done for us. You never know when there is a Rahab close by who is longing to hear about a Savior. It could be your story that causes lasting transformation. What a powerful impact to have!

Pondering Thoughts:

What kind of stories do you tell about God? What is your testimony? If you had to give a 30-second elevator testimony, what would you say? How would the things you spoke today change if you knew the whole world was listening?

Praise and Petitions:

Rabbi, Great Teacher, your wisdom is so far reaching from anything I could ever explain to others. But it is my prayer you will help me know what to say and what to tell in order to advance your plan for mankind. Please help me prepare the testimony you want to come from my lips. Guide me as I seek to tell the story of you in my life. I ask this in your name, Amen.

Prayer Journaling Notes:

Points from the Editor:

Thirty seconds isn't long enough! After the loss of the greatest sources of strength I'd ever known on the face of this earth, I struggled to depend on God in a new way. That I didn't feel victimized was nothing short of God's loving hand covering my eyes, head, and heart. If you want to know what it is that captivates your heart in the life of another believer, ask the believer. The impact is already a result, but get close enough to know what makes the believer tick. And let people who are drawn to you get close enough too. Let them inside. You don't have to glorify the details of dark places to glorify the God who changed you into His likeness. If you let someone get close enough to see you, he/she will capture your imperfections. In doing so he/she will see your authenticity - the real you. And he/she will love you even more. God will be glorified.

Questions and Reflections:

1. What stood out to you in the scripture reading today?

2. Answer at least one of the pondering questions?

3. Personalize the prayer for your own life below:

DAY 22

Scripture Reading: Matthew 1: 1-5

Rahab's life changed in so many ways when those walls came down that day. But one significant way in which she changed was in her lifestyle. She was a harlot when the spies met her; afterwards she was mentioned as a wife to Salmon. Some Jewish historians say Salmon was actually one of the spies. We don't know this for sure, but what we do know is Salmon was from the tribe of Judah. For Rahab to go from being a woman of such ill repute to a woman married into the tribe of Judah is significant. God definitely performed more than one miracle in this story. Perhaps you feel today you are tarnished or without help and hope. Look at Rahab. Take notice of what God did specifically for her. He is no respecter of persons.

Pondering Thoughts:

God changes our stories mid-stream when we make a covenant with Him. What story has God changed for you? What would you like for God to change about your story? How will you reach out to Him to ask for His intervention in your life?

Praise and Petitions:

God, who taketh vengeance, I give you honor and reverence. I know you are Lord of all the earth, and while mankind seemingly moves further from you and your plans for us each day, I want to be someone upon whom you can depend. Help me adjust as you make changes in my life. Show me your ways, so I may walk with you. I ask in your name, Amen.

Prayer Journaling Notes:

Points from the Editor:

God is the great Redeemer of the past. We cannot pretend it did not happen. We can't lie or hide. He intends to use who we were in whom we are today and in our future. Better than we can fathom, He is the great reacher-back. He can reach back into our past, grab what He can take for His glory, and straight up slap Satan in the face with it. I've seen Him do it, haven't you? It's why the enemy can be our footstool, and His footstool. Satan is under our feet. His future is frightful. Ours is wrapped up in the one faithful God who can use anything for His good and glory. Don't forget your past, but do forgive yourself just as Christ forgave you. How clean does that feel?

Questions and Reflections:

1. What stood out to you in the scripture reading today?

2. Answer at least one of the pondering questions?

3. Personalize the prayer for your own life below:

DAY 23

Scripture Reading: Matthew 1: 6-10

Rahab, who became the wife of Salmon, had a child. That child's name was Boaz. And from that we know Boaz had a child named Obed. Obed had a little boy named Jesse, and then we have the little boy named David from Jesse. Rahab was David's great-great grandmother. From harlot to grandmother of a king, Rahab definitely changed her outcome in life. How did she go from ill repute to royalty? God changed her direction in life, and she migrated to the people who would introduce her to the God of second chances. That is pretty amazing.

Pondering Thoughts:

How has God proven Himself to you in your life? Think of a time when you needed a second chance. How did God intervene for you?

Praise and Petitions:

Root of David, you are amazing in how you can make the seemingly unimportant people become royalty. How you do that, I do not understand, but I am so thankful you do. Help me to see the royalty you see in others. Help me to give the second chances when they are needed for others as you have given them to me. I ask this in your name, Amen.

Prayer Journaling Notes:

Points from the Editor:

God is not in a hurry. He doesn't have to be. He created and owns time from the first tick; He is timeless. He is not bound by it, but it bows to Him. It took generations to bring forth the child who would save the world. Many more will live and die before we see the Messiah return. The best thing we can do to help God is to cooperate with Him. We get weary in the wait when He wants us to worship instead. We stand and proclaim our will when all He wanted was us to bow to His - sooner rather than later. It's time to throw up the white flag of surrender. If you already have done that, then do the next thing He calls you to do. If not, what in the world are you waiting for? It's your turn, and it's time to turn.

Questions and Reflections:

1. What stood out to you in the scripture reading today?

2. Answer at least one of the pondering questions?

3. Personalize the prayer for your own life below:

DAY 24

Scripture Reading: Matthew 1: 11-15

Rahab was saved because of her faith in the God of the Israelites. She had not been raised as a Hebrew (Jew or Israelite). She was from Jericho. Her name was derived from Egypt, and contained the name of Ra, a god of Egypt. Yet, she heard something. She believed something. She longed for something. She wanted more. She wanted more from men than the visits to her home to use her. She wanted a relationship and a family. Rahab wanted to intimately know this God who had caused the courage of her people to fail. She believed in Him. Because of her belief and her ability to ask for the right covenant with the Israelite spies, she and her family were saved.

Pondering Thoughts:

Faith is so important. It is important for us to instill faith in our children. How does your faith in God measure up today? Where does your faith show strength? Where are weaknesses in your faith? Faith is critical. Strengthen your faith today.

Praise and Petitions:

God, who is rich in mercy, thank you for giving every person a measure of faith. Help me to exercise my faith. Show me how to grow in faith in you as well as in your plan for my life. I ask this in your name, Amen.

Prayer Journaling Notes:

Points from the Editor:

Eternity is set in the heart of man. It was surely in Rahab's heart there was something better. She got to experience a fraction of that on earth. Her faith catapulted her to a place she thought she'd never be. It was unfathomable. She was used and used up. She continued to practice sin, but something on the inside compelled her to risk her life to save spies. Why? God had her number more than any man had her address. He spared her impending doom. He is alway the initiator. Just when we think we chose Him, we come to understand He was the One who came to court us, to draw us, to completely capture our raging and rebellious hearts for His purposes. Never ever think a person who is not saved cannot be God's instrument. Never think a believer cannot be used by Satan. Let God use you the way He used Rahab and determine to be a difference maker.

Questions and Reflections:

1. What stood out to you in the scripture reading today?

2. Answer at least one of the pondering questions?

3. Personalize the prayer for your own life below:

DAY 25

Scripture Reading: Matthew 1: 16-20

Rahab was justified by her works. She knew simply to believe in the God of the Israelites was not enough. When God's spies requested protection and safety, she provided it. She also provided them with a way to escape, securing her own escape from the judgment God was about to hand down to Jericho for its idolatry. We would do well to learn faith is not the only requirement in our Christian walk, but our faith is made perfect by our works. When God speaks to our hearts or requires some action from us, we need to act quickly. Rahab acted immediately because of her faith in God, and her works or actions made her faith perfect before an Almighty God.

Pondering Thoughts:

What has God impressed upon you to do for Him? When is it most difficult for you to respond immediately? Our faith relies on our works (or actions), and it is so easy to hold back, afraid to move. How can we best prepare for times when God requires our immediate movement?

Praise and Petitions:

God, who is blessed forever, I praise you. I want the actions of my life to please you. I know there are times when I hold back, or I don't move expediently. Help me to fully trust you and move when you require actions of me. I ask this in your name, Amen.

Prayer Journaling Notes:

Points from the Editor:

Don't be overwhelmed when God gives you something to do. Don't overthink it. Just do the first thing. Then do the next thing. He provides the time if we will sacrifice the reservations in our hearts - the questions and debates. Wonderings often produce wandering, and then we look back and are confused about how we became so distant. God is the great delegator. He knows how and why your very life works into His mosaic, His grand scheme. It's for you. He is for you. He planned it all along - before you were ever born.

Questions and Reflections:

1. What stood out to you in the scripture reading today?

2. Answer at least one of the pondering questions?

3. Personalize the prayer for your own life below:

DAY 26

Scripture Reading: Matthew 1: 21-25

Rahab not only becomes a part of the tribe of Judah; she becomes a direct ancestor to Joseph, Jesus' earthly father. While we know Joseph was not Jesus' biological father, this does not negate the importance of Joseph's role in Jesus' life. Jesus is called the Lion of Judah, and from Salmon and Rahab, this lineage derives. This is such a great honor to a woman who most of society would not bestow such kindness. God chooses to reward her faith and works by placing her in the direct line to Jesus' earthly genealogy. What an honor! That scarlet cord continued to flow metaphorically all the way to Calvary as a gesture of salvation to those who believe.

Pondering Thoughts:

How blessed do you feel because you are grafted into the family of God? While we may not be Jewish or Hebrew, God has allowed us to be sons and daughters of the King of Kings. We are joint-heirs with Christ, and He is still preparing a place for us. How does this make you feel to know the King of Glory loves you this much?

Praise and Petitions:

Thou, who my soul loveth, I thank you for your kinship to me. I am not worthy, but you have adopted me anyway. I am so blessed to be called a child of God. I can never give you adequate praise or service. Help me to be the child I should be and to grow the Kingdom. I want to be of service to you. I ask this in your name, Amen.

Prayer Journaling Notes:

Points from the Editor:

It's true. I'm royalty, and so are you. I want my crown, and I'll get it one day. In a little girl's heart, she often dreams about being a princess. Then, one day, she gets to be one. She was all along, but she didn't know it. So she dressed up and pretended. It was so real. Life has a way of making us wonder what happened to those dreams, but God knows the reality of heaven and His Kingdom. It's real. We'll all sit at the banqueting table. Then Christ Himself will serve us. I believe it with every ounce of my being.

Questions and Reflections:

1. What stood out to you in the scripture reading today?

2. Answer at least one of the pondering questions?

3. Personalize the prayer for your own life below:

DAY 27

Scripture Reading: 1 Peter 2: 1-5

In these final few days, I want to discuss some prevailing themes in the life story of Rahab. Today I want to talk about her courage. She was an amazing example of how to act courageously with the enemy all around her. She did not give in to the pressure of her peers, and she stood bravely for God when it counted most. Courage was important in Biblical times, but it is equally significant in our own time. We should pray for courage daily. The warfare may be different; the weapons may not be the same. However, we are bombarded daily by an evil adversary who would like to do nothing more than destroy us. Take courage. Be brave. You can do this!

Pondering Thoughts:

On a scale of 1-10, how would you rate your bravery in fighting the enemy of your soul? What are some things you can do to increase your courage? Give an example of someone who have proven to be courageous to you.

Praise and Petitions:

Thou, preserver of men, I thank you for the ability to completely trust you. I know we have an adversary, and there are times when he makes things look impossible. But I also know if I can have courage, you will save me. Please help me have the kind of courage Rahab showed there in Jericho. Help me completely trust in you in all circumstances of my life. I ask this in your name, Amen.

Prayer Journaling Notes:

Points from the Editor:

The author has hit on another of my personal core values. This is what faith looks like to me from a Biblical perspective:

Lord, I not only believe in you, but I believe you. You are who you say you are. You can do what you say you can do. I am who you say I am, and I can do all things through Christ who is my strength. Your word is alive and active in me (taken from Believing God by Beth Moore). Because of this faith, I am willing and available, but also obedient to follow your Spirit's lead in my life, no matter how small or large the task. I am investing 15-20 minutes per day in my walk with you by scripture reading and memory.

Questions and Reflections:

1. What stood out to you in the scripture reading today?

2. Answer at least one of the pondering questions?

3. Personalize the prayer for your own life below:

DAY 28

Scripture Reading: 1 Peter 2: 6-10

The second theme I found interesting in Rahab's story was trust. Trust in this story was two-fold. The spies had to trust Rahab; Rahab had to trust the spies. I believe in our Christian walk we must learn to trust, but we must also become trustworthy. Rahab had to place her complete trust Joshua would honor her plea for her family's safety. We have to learn to trust God with our families. We must do our part, and then let God do His. This isn't easy, and it couldn't have been easy for Rahab either. But she did it, and so can we.

Pondering Thoughts:

Where do you have the most difficulties trusting God in your life? Why do you think it is difficult trusting Him in those areas? What can you do to help you built your trust in God?

Praise and Petitions:

The Invisible God, I praise you though I can't see you. I know you exist, though I cannot touch you. There are times in my life I do wonder and become afraid. Help me to overcome those times and learn to completely trust you. I cannot do this alone: I, like Rahab, need a token. Please send me a token of assurance along the way. I ask this in your name, Amen.

Prayer Journaling Notes:

Points from the Editor:

Trusting is hard. It was for David. But the great psalmist beautifully penned words straight from his heart to God's. These words brought life to his own soul, and reminded him of God's faithfulness and trustworthiness. Psalm 3: "But you, Lord, are a shield around me, my glory, the one who lifes my head high. I call to the Lord, and He answers me from His holy mountain. I lie down and sleep; I wake again, because the Lord sustains me. I will not fear though tens of thousands assail me on every side." If trusting God is hard enough, it's even tougher to follow Him in such a way He would count us as ones to be trusted. He holds the trustworthy ones to a standard that requires our very best effort and character. 1 Corinthians 4:2: "Now it is required that those who have been given a trust must prove faithful."

Questions and Reflections:

1. What stood out to you in the scripture reading today?

2. Answer at least one of the pondering questions?

3. Personalize the prayer for your own life below:

DAY 29

Scripture Reading: 1 Peter 2: 11-15

The third theme I found in this story of Rahab is the true meaning of a covenant. Rahab did her part; the spies did their part. They kept the covenant they had made with each other. In the day and age in which we live, it seems like people are not too concerned with covenants anymore. If they don't like an agreement, they simply look for a legal way out of it. As Christians, we should take great care before we enter into covenants with others. And we should never enter a binding covenant with the escape clause in mind. God makes everlasting covenants, and we should strive to be more like Him.

Pondering Thoughts:

Do you have an example of a covenant you entered where you wish you had not? How did you handle this covenant? There are many examples of covenants: relationships, jobs, contracts, legal documents, etc. Yet, so often we start feeling trapped and want out. What would be your advice to someone who is about to enter a covenant with another person, firm, or business?

Praise and Petitions:

Rock of my refuge, I know your covenants are everlasting, and I can bank on them. There have been times I have failed with covenants I have made. Help me to keep my commitments and to be careful entering into commitments you do not feel I should partake. I ask this in your name, Amen.

Prayer Journaling Notes:

Points from the Editor:

The scripture reading from today's devotion stands out to me, especially verse 15: "For it is God's will that by doing good you should silence the ignorant talk of foolish people." A life characterized by mostly good works can often disguise a filthy heart. But the most important covenant we will ever make is the one we make to God when we give Him the entrance He deserves into our hearts. He sits enthroned upon my imperfect heart. I serve Him blamelessly every day I live, not because I am perfect, but because He is. I keep my sins confessed up to date. His discipline and severe mercy when I continue practicing sin will further wound my broken soul, to the point I will come to understand the covenant was also broken with Him. His, however, remains. He wraps His arms around me. He takes me in. He does it again and again, each time making my wandering heart less prone to do so, less likely to slip too far away.

Questions and Reflections:

1. What stood out to you in the scripture reading today?

2. Answer at least one of the pondering questions?

3. Personalize the prayer for your own life below:

DAY 30

Scripture Reading: 1 Peter 2: 16 - 20

The fourth theme I found in Rahab's story involves change. Rahab had to prepare for drastic changes in her life. She would have to forsake what she had known all her days and become part of a foreign people. Yet, Rahab knew this was necessary in order for her to survive. Change is going to come. It always does. Some changes are for the better; other changes leave us feeling forsaken and sorrowful. Know when God requires a change in our lives, He will help us make the adjustments. He had Salmon waiting to help Rahab; He will send help to you, even if He has to dispatch angels to bring it to you. Get ready. Change happens, and it happens often in our lives.

Pondering Thoughts:

What are some changes you have had to make since you started your walk with God? How have those changes had an impact on your life? When you know or sense a change is coming, what do you do to prepare?

Praise and Petitions:

The Lamb, you made the ultimate change by coming to earth from your throne in Heaven to lay your life down for me. If you could do such an act of love and mercy for me, surely I can make a few adaptations for you when required. Help me to know how to best revise my life in order to please you more each day. I ask this in your name, Amen.

Prayer Journaling Notes:

Points from the Editor:

Change - some like it, some don't. Growing up, my family moved about every four years. My dad was a petroleum engineer, and we made our way around those regions. My sister disclosed years later to me, even after marrying, she would get itchy for a change or move every 4-5 years. Personally, when I get comfortable I will bear misery and minor inconveniences or frustrations just to escape even the thought of change. It's worse as I've gotten older. I think it always is harder for older people. But right now, God has brought change to me. Job change. Financial change. Ministry change. He is using these changes to pick me up from where I have been long enough. He wants me somewhere else, and I get that. I just don't know where. It will be foreign to me, like it was to Rahab. But it will be God's plan, and I will trust Him.

Questions and Reflections:

1. What stood out to you in the scripture reading today?

2. Answer at least one of the pondering questions?

3. Personalize the prayer for your own life below:

DAY 31

Scripture Reading: 1 Peter 2: 21-25

The final theme I want to discuss from the life of Rahab was chance. God gave Rahab a second chance because He desired to do something phenomenal with her life. While we have discussed how God is a God of second chances, when we do have a change or opportunity to make a difference, we should do everything within our power to make it happen. People need us to take the risk. God calls us to leave our box of safety in order to change the world. It is perilous at times. It may even be dangerous, but remember if He requires it, He'll see us through the challenges we face. Take the risk; calculate the costs. But remember, it is your Creator who summons you to do the unimaginable.

Pondering Thoughts:

How have you taken risks for God in the past? What did you find most difficult about taking the risk? What would you do if you woke up tomorrow and God said, "It's time to do something turbulent but necessary for the Kingdom?"

Praise and Petitions:

Strength to the poor, it is because of the chance you took on humanity I have the opportunity to spend eternity with you in Heaven. I want to be a risk-taker for you. I know I often shy away from risks, and I feel very inadequate, but if you call me to do it, help me to go the distance. I ask this in your name, Amen.

Prayer Journaling Notes:

Points from the Editor:

With some recent changes in my life requiring risk and taking a chance, God has changed my perspective. He constantly pushes me out there and says, "What do you have to lose?" He's right. I've come to realize in taking risks I have everything to gain. He's writing a story in the risk that includes His glory.

The Wait Is Over
What are you waiting for now? This thing He is doing is part of His vow.
He's writing a story; it includes His glory.
He's telling me softly; this thing is too lofty.
It's not meant for my kingdom, not for your lingerings.
I'm ready to use it; get ready to lose it.
Not yours anymore; now mine ever more.
You can trust it to me; just close your eyes and believe.
You've done your part; now let me do mine.

Questions and Reflections:

1. What stood out to you in the scripture reading today?

2. Answer at least one of the pondering questions?

3. Personalize the prayer for your own life below:

June
Miriam - The Musician

*Scripture Reading - Verses associated with Miriam's life,
Psalms 3 and Ecclesiastes 3 & 4*

There is no doubt in my mind; Miriam was a great warrior princess. She was given the gift of prophesy, and she takes her place in Jewish history as one of the three great shepherds of Israel. She proved to be wise beyond her years in helping her mother protect her baby brother, and she led the women in song during their deliverance and through the wilderness. Miriam made mistakes during her life, but God proved to be faithful to her despite her errors in judgment and the jealousy that would creep into her life during her later years.

According to Jewish history, God gave Miriam the special gift of providing water for the Israelites. Much of her life was surrounded by stories of how she interacted with water: the Nile, the Red Sea, and the well and rock that traveled with the Israelites. Her timbrel was used to bring much encouragement to the women in the wilderness. Her story is intriguing, filled with prophecy and pain. Join me as I explore the history of this fascinating sister: the older sister of Moses, prophetess and poetess of Israel.

DAY 1

Scripture Reading: Exodus 15: 1-5

Miriam was born in the land of Goshen as a Hebrew slave in Egypt. Her family had been relocated to Egypt during the great famine prophesied by Joseph, and this was the only land she knew. Miriam grew up knowing the hardships of serving Pharaoh. No doubt she heard her father and mother discuss the awful conditions of the Jewish people many times. Even though they were God's chosen people, they were in bondage, and they needed a deliverer. I can only imagine how little Miriam felt each day she rose from sleep hoping today would be the day for deliverance. We all have areas of bondage in our lives; some more than others. There is something within the heart of a person that wants to be free. God brings freedom and deliverance. Just hold on.

Pondering Thoughts:

What kind of bondage have you experienced in your life? What areas of bondage still exist today? What are the hopes and dreams you have for your life or perhaps the lives of family or friends in bondage.

Praise and Petitions:

Chief Cornerstone, I thank you for your deliverance. I praise you for the freedom you give to your children. Help me to break free from the chains the devil would send my way. I know you break every chain binding your children. I ask this in your name, Amen.

Prayer Journaling Notes:

Points from the Editor:

We need to be delivered, mostly from ourselves. George Bernard Shaw is quoted: "This is the true joy in life, the being used for a purpose recognized by yourself as a mighty one; the being a force of nature instead of a feverish, selfish little clot of ailments and grievances complaining the world will not devote itself to making you happy." So many times the bondage I face in life is centered around my own selfish and sinful nature. I am addicted to approval, in bondage to my self-imposed deadlines, chained to my guilt about all the "shoulds" in life. I should entertain more. I should keep my house more spotless, cook more, not be so lazy, and not waste so much time. But when I am all wrapped up in my Deliverer, I realize He's the One who carries me, picks me up, and places His worth on me just as I am. It's quite liberating to be rescued from myself by my Deliverer.

Questions and Reflections:

1. What stood out to you in the scripture reading today?

2. Answer at least one of the pondering questions?

3. Personalize the prayer for your own life below:

DAY 2

Scripture Reading: Exodus 15: 6 -10

Miriam was the older sister of Moses, and historians say she was about seven years old when she watched over her brother among the bulrushes of the Nile. This child had already seen so very much in her life by this time. It is truly a miracle she as well as other children survived under the harshness of Pharaoh. Jewish history tells us by this time Miriam had already received her gift of prophecy and used it to guide her family in Egypt. Many times we see children as too young to be used by God. Miriam is an excellent example of how wrong we can be. Never underestimate how God can use a child.

Pondering Thoughts:

Think of a child you feel has been given a special gift. What makes that child special? Think back to your own childhood. Was there ever a time you felt God nudging you or preparing you? If so, write your thoughts on that experience. How can we adults help foster the spirit of greatness in children?

Praise and Petitions:

Deliverer, you proved your power to Miriam in her life, and you continually prove your power to me. I praise you for each time you deliver me and my family in our difficulties. I ask you help me look for others who I can help through the harshness in life. I ask this in your name, Amen.

Prayer Journaling Notes:

Points from the Editor:

Parents, above anyone in the church or school, hold the greatest empowering influence over their children. As parents, we often misjudge the age at which a child's spiritual tendencies are really even there. Children play so much, but they miss so little. The things you don't want to catch their attention do. The things you really wish they were drawn to fail you. All the while, they are watching and listening. The earlier they capture the idea of being used for a purpose greater than themselves, the more likely they are to step into that role long-term for the glory of God. Whatever we get first from our parents, and from their modeling, is often what sticks. No pressure, right? If your hope is they will be used, then get busy being used yourself. That's how it happens.

Questions and Reflections:

1. What stood out to you in the scripture reading today?

2. Answer at least one of the pondering questions?

3. Personalize the prayer for your own life below:

DAY 3

Scripture Reading: Exodus 15: 11 - 15

Miriam carefully watched for her brother from the bulrushes. What dedication this child had to her mother and her brother. Pharaoh demanded the death of all male children, but Miriam kept a watchful eye so she could help her mother save her brother. Surely by this time in her life she had witnessed the cruelty of Pharaoh and the Egyptians towards her people. I'm certain she was aware of the danger in hiding this baby, yet such love and devotion forced her to put her life in danger for her family. While the plan to save Moses was risky, Miriam did what she could to help her mother keep from losing her baby to death. Please try to remember, this child was only about seven years old.

Pondering Thoughts:

I can only imagine the training Israelites gave their children even at the earliest age in order for them to survive. What are we providing to our children today in terms of spiritual training and survival? How do you train your children or the children in your family for spiritual growth? What is important in your home, or your family?

Praise and Petitions:

Gracious and Merciful God, I thank you for giving us understanding and knowledge. I know we are supposed to train our children, and I certainly want to do my part. Help me to know what to say and how to say it in order to instill your truth into my children, grandchildren, and others I know. I ask this in your name, Amen.

Prayer Journaling Notes:

Points from the Editor:

Godly parenting happens on Sundays... Mondays, Tuesdays, Wednesdays, Thursdays, Fridays, and Saturdays. It happens at bedtime, at mealtime, and at homework time (especially when prayer is required to focus and make the grade). It happens during sibling rivalries, meanness, manipulation, laziness, and disrespect. Every moment... Every lesson. They are not babies as long as we think. They learn so quickly. Their little minds are blank slates every single day. They are the next generation's teachers, preachers, elders, deacons, and Godly remnant. We have no earthly idea who is sleeping in our beds at night. One thing is for sure - God knows, and He entrusts parents to do what only they can do. Grandparents are absolutely and equally important, but parents are not off the hook, not ever. The reward comes way later. The work is now.

Questions and Reflections:

1. What stood out to you in the scripture reading today?

2. Answer at least one of the pondering questions?

3. Personalize the prayer for your own life below:

DAY 4

Scripture Reading: Exodus 15: 16 - 20

Miriam waited by the bulrushes for her brother's fate. At seven, Miriam may not have fully understood the low probability of her brother's survival. However, Jewish history tells us Miriam had already prophesied her mother would have a son who would be the leader of Israel and would save them from the slavery of Egypt. Aaron was already born, so he was not the intended recipient of the prophecy. But this child... This little baby in the basket... He must be the one. And she guarded him with all her might. The Bible tells us in the last days prophecies will go forth like never before upon all flesh, sons and daughters. We should be preparing our children to be recipients of the gifts of prophecies and dreams.

Pondering Thoughts:

How would you react if a child gave you a word of prophecy? Would you tend to look at the child in disbelief? What kinds of limitations do we tend to place on God and whom or what He can use in our lives?

Praise and Petitions:

Immanuel, you are forever with us, just as you were with Miriam and Moses on the Nile. Help me to remember you are ever present and care about my needs as well as the preservation of my family. I pray for protection over my family each day. I ask this in your name, Amen.

Prayer Journaling Notes:

Points from the Editor:

Have you ever wondered why Jesus tells us we must have faith like a child to enter heaven? Think about children in the Bible to whom God spoke so clearly. Mary was really just a child. Samuel, Joseph, Daniel, and his friends... These are just a few we know. A child listens, is less distracted, and very often has greater faith, untainted by the struggles of the world. Sometimes the child is the only one listening to God in a family full of adults who really need to be. I believe the innocence of a child can often attract the heart of God where sin is not so present. Yes, we are all born into sin, and we all have a sinful nature. But the tenderness of a child - a child's love, prayer, and joy must please our God enough to speak to them and through them. We may never know it, but when they do what seems to be wise, I wonder if God spoke to them.

Questions and Reflections:

1. What stood out to you in the scripture reading today?

2. Answer at least one of the pondering questions?

3. Personalize the prayer for your own life below:

DAY 5

Scripture Reading: Exodus 15: 21 - 27

We are not told how long Miriam had to wait along the Nile with Moses in the basket, but soon there was an unexpected visitor - the daughter of Pharaoh. Miriam was able to watch her prophecy come to pass right before her little eyes. The princess of Egypt need only place claim on the baby to rescue him from impending death. Isn't it odd God sent the woman whose father demanded for Moses to die to save him? What a smart and brave little girl Miriam must have been to approach the princess with an immediate solution for baby Moses and his physical needs.

Pondering Thoughts:

How well are we training our children for the spiritual battles ahead? If it was your responsibility to train a little Miriam, how would you do it? Where are we missing the opportunities to train our children in our churches? Where are we doing well?

Praise and Petitions:

King of Glory, I praise you for the children you place in our lives. I ask you to help me train them for the work you want accomplished for the Kingdom. Help me to see the need to work with children and visualize their place in your plans for the church. I ask this in your name, Amen.

Prayer Journaling Notes:

Points from the Editor:

My daughter used to come into Ladies' Bible Study with me for the first 30 minutes because we started earlier than the children's Sunday night activities. She wanted to help; she would put things on the white board standing on a chair. She would listen to us as we did prayer requests. We were not deep into the study or discussion while she was present, but she got it. When the time came to help with VBS years later as a teenager, she jumped right in. She felt compelled to lead her cheer squad in nightly camp devotions without any prompting or suggesting from anyone. Children can and will see a need and offer to be a solution. They may need mentoring and guidance, but they can be entrusted to serve God young if they want to. And they do. Lots of them just want the chance to serve.

Questions and Reflections:

1. What stood out to you in the scripture reading today?

2. Answer at least one of the pondering questions?

3. Personalize the prayer for your own life below:

DAY 6

Scripture Reading: Numbers 12: 1 - 5

Miriam proposed to the princess to find a nursemaid for little Moses. The princess instructed her to find someone, so she took Moses back to his mother. Jochebed nursed him until he was weaned and returned back to the princess. I am sure there were many days when Miriam brought Moses to and from the princess to her mother. It is likely she watched her mother have to release her brother back to a woman who was part of the family who enslaved her people. This had to be heartbreaking for Jochebed, Miriam, and the entire family. Yet, this family took this precious time as an opportunity to train little Moses. He might have to live in the house of Pharaoh, but Moses would know he was in fact a Hebrew.

Pondering Thoughts:

How would you respond if you had to send your child into the enemy's home daily? How do you protect the values of your family with your children knowing they are bombarded by anti-Christian values daily? What can we do to build a barrier around our children?

Praise and Petitions:

Jesus Christ, the Righteous, thank you for caring for children. You made it very vocal in your earthly ministry you care deeply for children. Help me to seek to train children for the Kingdom. Help me to look at each soul as a priceless part of your plan. I ask this in your name, Amen.

Prayer Journaling Notes:

Points from the Editor:

Surely Miriam never forgot God's divine hand and mysterious ways in this that took place. What a lesson right on the pages of her life! Her responsibility was monumental for just a child. Children learn how to be good moms and dads by doing those things that help their moms and dads - babysitting, bottle feeding, playing, entertaining, toting, & consoling. She was a mighty-sized sister for a God-sized purpose. To think God planned this good work for her before the creation of the world is unimaginable. But He did. My heart knows He has done it since then time and again. For that I am thankful.

Questions and Reflections:

1. What stood out to you in the scripture reading today?

2. Answer at least one of the pondering questions?

3. Personalize the prayer for your own life below:

DAY 7

Scripture Reading: Numbers 12: 6 - 10

Miriam was at least seven years older than Moses. If you have siblings, you are either the older or younger sibling, and depending on your place in the family, you may have different responsibilities. While I am actually a middle child of my father's children, I am the oldest raised in my home with my mother. I will have to say I felt extreme responsibility for my younger sister through the years. You want to protect those who are younger; it is a natural feeling. I'm quite sure Miriam's place as the older sibling proved to be quite frustrating for her at times. She had an enormous responsibility to protect her younger brothers in a very harsh land. What a little warrior!

Pondering Thoughts:

I often think I failed my little sister many times. There are things that happened in her life from which I could not protect her. I wish I would have been able to do so. But in others areas I was able to do so. For those times, I feel successful as a sister. When have you been vulnerable as an older, younger, or only child? If you were the older sibling, how have you protected your younger siblings? If you are younger, how were you protected by older siblings? If you were an only child, when could you have used the protection of an older sibling?

Praise and Petitions:

Majesty on High, I thank you for protection of our children. Help me to always protect and never put a child in harm's way. I ask this in your name, Amen.

Prayer Journaling Notes:

Points from the Editor:

We have protection from an older Brother. According to scripture, Christ Himself is our older Brother who experienced suffering to bring many sons to glory. I picture Him wrapping His arm around my back shoulders and walking side-by-side with me up to His Father, standing beside me and telling the Father - "Here's one more of your children, covered by my blood, protected evermore from the evil one; she's with me." One thing I've learned, love always protects. It's pure love's first response. I've learned it the only way I probably could, by God teaching me during the rough spots. Sometimes the protecting kind of love covers a multitude of sin. Sometimes it fights hell and demonic forces for the sake of the weakest link. Other times protecting love sits quietly by, knowing only the Holy Spirit can do what must be done. But this I know - all the time love that protects is praying love.

Questions and Reflections:

1. What stood out to you in the scripture reading today?

2. Answer at least one of the pondering questions?

3. Personalize the prayer for your own life below:

DAY 8

Scripture Reading: Numbers 12: 11 - 16

Miriam's name has two specific meanings in Hebrew: (1) bitterness, and (2) rebellious. It is likely Amram and Jochebed had much bitterness when Miriam was born. They were slaves in Egypt, and it was harsh for Hebrews under the new Pharaoh who did not remember Joseph or all he had done for Egypt. To name a child "bitterness" or "rebellion" shows the deep frustration that must be felt in the hearts of parents. It is amazing God used this little girl to prophesy Israel would be freed and joyful again in the Promised Land. Though her name may have meant sorrowful things in the present, her prophecy told of a better time for all of Israel when they would be free once again with the lands promised to their father Abraham as their new home.

Pondering Thoughts:

While we do experience sorrow in our lives, we must always look for hope in the future. When have you experienced deep sorrow in your own life? How have you looked forward to the future when God will turn your sorrow into dancing and joy?

Praise and Petitions:

Only Begotten Son of God, you experienced deep sorrow while you were on earth. Yet, you knew eventually sorrow would turn into rejoicing. Help me to remember weeping only lasts for a little while, and one day all my sorrows will turn into joy if I remain faithful to you. I ask this in your name, Amen.

Prayer Journaling Notes:

Points from the Editor:

We could not physically bear pure joy all the time. Our bodies would not hold up. Conversely, if we never understood pain and suffering, we would not truly appreciate joy and happiness. The Bible tells us if we do not share in the sufferings of Christ, we do not truly know Him. Part of the reason He had to endure them is so He would sympathize with ours. Every minute of suffering seems to last an hour. It lays heavy on the soul, mind, and body - at times it seems unbearable. We breathe through it, cry through it, hide through it, reason through it, and even punish ourselves through it. Often we decide we deserve it somehow, and guilt is an age old tool of a longtime enemy. Other times, we shake our fist at the part of God we think is unfair - the God we believe has heaped this thing on us. In the end, we are relieved to know it's true. All of us deserved death on a cross, but our Savior took it all for us so we only experience a fraction of it.

Questions and Reflections:

1. What stood out to you in the scripture reading today?

2. Answer at least one of the pondering questions?

3. Personalize the prayer for your own life below:

DAY 9

Scripture Reading: Numbers 20: 1- 5

Miriam's adult life remains somewhat a mystery, yet historians say she had a direct connection to Hur, the warrior who held up the hands of Moses with Aaron. Josephus, the Jewish historian, tells us she was married to Hur, while other biblical and Jewish historians believe Hur was actually her son with her husband, who some believe was none other than Caleb. Whether Hur was her husband or son, Miriam had enough influence in his life for him to realize helping Moses was essential for the survival of the Hebrew nation. Well into her eighties or nineties, Miriam was still looking after Moses, her baby brother. She instilled the hope of the Jews within her family.

Pondering Thoughts:

What have I done... what have you done... to ensure the hope of Christ in our families? How well are we building soldiers for the Cross? When I look at my family, it pains me greatly when I do not see soldiers in God's army. I need to do more. What about you? What can we do to raise up a Godly army in the future?

Praise and Petitions:

Redeemer, I praise you for your redemption of my soul. I thank you for caring for my family. I pray the blessings of God over my children and grandchildren. I know the stakes are high for the safety of their souls. Help me to pray ever more earnestly for their salvation. I ask this in your name, Amen.

Prayer Journaling Notes:

Points from the Editor:

We've never paid our dues with serving God. Miriam may have been the one little girl who saved a brother who saved a nation of God's chosen people. Wasn't that enough? But as an old song goes, "He paid a debt He did not owe; I owed a debt I could not pay." I'll never give enough of myself to a God I can never out give. One day I will stand before Him with tears because I will wish I had done more, then He will wipe away every tear and will give me a promised eternity in fellowship with Him free of sin and death. Miriam understood you just never give up or give in. Love never fails, and every act of love we show to our families is like fruit on a tree never falling to the ground. It drops straight into the hands of the Master Gardener. It's the fruit bearing His name for His glory. It's the fruit producing a legacy making His name famous. It's sweet and is rewarded in eternity.

Questions and Reflections:

1. What stood out to you in the scripture reading today?

2. Answer at least one of the pondering questions?

3. Personalize the prayer for your own life below:

DAY 10

Scripture Reading: Numbers 20: 6 - 10

Miriam was the first woman in the Scriptures to be called a prophetess. This was truly a great honor for her, and a great honor for women. We, too, have a place in the Kingdom to serve and to lead. In this battle between God and His mortal enemy, Satan, we do not have to sit on the sidelines. We, as women, can too have a purpose and a place in this fight. God seeks for vessels willing to be used. Miriam made herself available to God, and we must make ourselves available as well. Our purposes may not be the same, but each of us is important to God. Our talents are not only desired, but required.

Pondering Thoughts:

How are you preparing yourself for your position in the Army of God? What have you done to show you are well trained and ready for God's battle cry in your life? What gifts have you been given? How are you using them?

Praise and Petitions:

Strength of Israel, I listen ever so closely for your calling. I don't want to miss a single thing you have planned for my life. Help me to rise when you want me to rise, and help me to watch and be ready when you call me. Don't allow me to become a hinderance in your work. I ask this in your name, Amen.

Prayer Journaling Notes:

Points from the Editor:

Someone else will step to the plate if we don't. Someone else will be blessed instead of us when we shy back from our callings. God equips those He calls. Being prepared and ready is often done by on-the-job training. He doesn't call the already equipped. If we can handle our callings without Him and within the realm of our personal readiness, then our independence would out trump the dependence on God required to do anything of lasting value for His glory. Our dependence on God must always be the overriding factor and final resource in our service to Him. He doesn't need us. He doesn't need anything. He has within Himself everything completing Him - He's not missing anything. The naked truth is we are in desperate need of Him.

Questions and Reflections:

1. What stood out to you in the scripture reading today?

2. Answer at least one of the pondering questions?

3. Personalize the prayer for your own life below:

DAY 11

Scripture Reading: Numbers 20: 11 - 15

Miriam waited about 80 years before she saw the prophecy given to her come to fruition. That requires a lot of patience. Can you imagine how she must have felt year after year? Wondering if she had made a mistake? She watched Moses grow up in Pharaoh's home. She likely heard of his exile for 40 years. As her age slowly crept upon her, I wonder if she ever doubted what God had spoken through her at an early age. Surely her faith must have wavered at times; and yet, God proved Himself faithful to her and to her people. Moses was the leader; it was just going to happen in God's timing.

Pondering Thoughts:

Have you ever questioned God's timing? I sure have. Think back on your life to a time when you asked God to move, how did you respond when the answer wasn't immediate? After God answered a prayer, how did this help your faith in Him grow? Reminisce God's faithfulness to you. Remember His provisions. Recollect His promises.

Praise and Petitions:

Consuming Fire, I know your timing is perfect. Yet, my human instinct for protection, safety, and intervention wants immediate solutions. I need patience. Yet, I don't really want to pray for patience. Help me to be willing to wait when you want me to wait. Help me to see the necessity of moving at the right time. I ask this in your name, Amen.

Prayer Journaling Notes:

Points from the Editor:

Waiting is so difficult. It seems, though, the more I have to wait, the longer I can endure it with the fruit of the Spirit called patience. Patience grows within me. I see others practice it, and I am inspired. If they can practice patience, then I can. I am the most impatient in daily life. I talk to drivers who cannot hear me. I tell myself things like: Go the speed limit! Five miles over wouldn't hurt! Hurry up! I'm in a hurry - why are there double lines here? I can see just fine to pass. My car is fast.... I can do this real quick. Thank goodness I live and drive mostly on country roads with virtually no traffic (unless you count wildlife). We need to get more comfortable with clicking the cruise control at a reasonable pace in the hard places of life. Letting life play out in God's timing is always perfect timing.

Questions and Reflections:

1. What stood out to you in the scripture reading today?

2. Answer at least one of the pondering questions?

3. Personalize the prayer for your own life below:

DAY 12

Scripture Reading: Numbers 20: 16 - 20

Finally the day came, after much pain and suffering, and Moses stood at the Red Sea, stretched forth his hand, and the waters parted. Miriam, along with all of the Hebrew nation, journeyed through the parted sea towards freedom for the first time in over 400 years. Joseph was sold by his brothers into slavery, marking the beginning of the Hebrew nation in Egypt. Finally a Promised Land is in view. By this time, Miriam was at least 87 years old, maybe older. But finally she saw in her brother the fulfillment of her prophecy.

Pondering Thoughts:

Have you ever felt like God was going to do something, but you had to wait a long time for it to happen? How did you feel when it finally happened? What prayers are you praying today you hope to see answered by God? What are you doing to keep your faith renewed until the answer comes?

Praise and Petitions:

Great Shepherd of the Sheep, I thank you for every answered and unanswered prayer. I pray you help me keep the faith until I see results. I know I am often impatient, and I need help in that area of my life. Help me to show others you often answer, but just not when we expect it. I ask for your guidance and help today. I ask this in your name, Amen.

Prayer Journaling Notes:

Points from the Editor:

Finally is a word of relief. Relief after a long time - typically involving difficulty or delay. Sometimes the word is used as the last in a series of related events. This "finally" for Miriam and God's people marked the end of one long chapter, yet the beginning of another longer one - a rejoicing, a victory. When something long awaited finally happens, we sure do feel relieved, sometimes overjoyed and victorious.   A healing deserves celebration, not a focus on how bad the pain was. An accomplished goal deserves a next enabling step in the right direction, not a constant belaboring of the sacrifice it required to get there. We endure the times that require finality in our lives to propel us to the new place that is our future. It's where God is - He's there in a future waiting for us to leave our past events.

Questions and Reflections:

1. What stood out to you in the scripture reading today?

2. Answer at least one of the pondering questions?

3. Personalize the prayer for your own life below:

DAY 13

Scripture Reading: Numbers 20: 21 - 25

According to Jewish history, Miriam led the women in worship as well as in the Torah (Law of God) just as Moses and Aaron led the men. She had a great responsibility for an entire nation of people. Like the Godly influence of her mother, Jochebed, Miriam became the leader for the Israelite women as they journeyed towards their freedom. The time had finally come for the Israelites to be free, and it was as important as ever the women of this great nation have a leader. Miriam was God's choice for her time.

Pondering Thoughts:

How important do you feel it is for women of our age to have Godly leaders just as men do? Why? Think of someone you know who is a Godly leader for women. What makes her a Godly leader? What are some of the attributes she exhibits? What leadership attributes to you feel you have? How do you use them?

Praise and Petitions:

Judge of all the Earth, thank you for sending leadership to your people. Help me to not only receive instruction, but to also lead when you want me to do so. I want to devote my life to your cause, and only you can best determine how my talents may be used. I ask only to be used by you. I ask this in your name, Amen.

Prayer Journaling Notes:

Points from the Editor:

Women understand women. We are inspired by one another. We are accountable to one another. My goodness, we desperately need one another. We are also made in the image of God, and He chose to give us the tenderness of His character, the nurturing side. We can be so mean and harsh. We can become angry at men who do not understand us and are not wired like we are. But as women, we can be huge encouragers to one another. To lead is to cause a person to go with one by holding that person by the hand while moving forward. A leader is often simply an example for others to follow, one who takes initiative or takes charge or command of a situation. Not everyone wants to lead, and some leaders do so by serving more so than in any other way. Whatever your place in leadership, you have before you the ultimate servant - leader in Christ Himself.

Questions and Reflections:

1. What stood out to you in the scripture reading today?

2. Answer at least one of the pondering questions?

3. Personalize the prayer for your own life below:

DAY 14

Scripture Reading: Numbers 20: 26 - 29

Not only was Miriam recorded as the first prophetess in the Scriptures, she was also recorded as the first poetess. What an honor! It would seem as if her very soul exploded with song and praise for what God has done for her people. After so much pain and suffering, she could have become embittered after so many years, but after they pass through the Red Sea, the first encounter we have with Miriam is her leading all of the Israelite women in song and dance for all God had done for them. God had finally delivered His people, 430 years from His original promise, and Miriam was there to give Him praise.

Pondering Thoughts:

How do you respond when God does intervene for you? What are some ways in which you show your gratitude towards God? Have you ever written a song or poem? If so, write it down for your remembrance. If you have never written before, stop for a few minutes and just think about all God has done. Respond by recording your thoughts.

Praise and Petitions:

My High Tower, if I were to record all your mighty works in my life, there would not be enough paper. Yet so many times I fail to give you honor and praise. I ask you to help me remember your acts of kindness towards me. Help me be able to speak what is in my heart towards you. I ask this in your name, Amen.

Prayer Journaling Notes:

Points from the Editor:

I love to write; poems are something that come to me in a flash. If I don't journal it and get the words and phrases rolling around in my head out and onto paper, almost immediately it is gone. Poetry can be therapy. It's another gift God gave Miriam. Sometimes just journaling gets us through treacherous places in life - at least it helps. If you are compelled to write, then hurry up! Stop talking about it, put a pen in your hand (or get your fingers on a keyboard), and get after it. If you don't know where to start, get a blank page out and write down the first word you sense God speaking to you. The rest will come.

Questions and Reflections:

1. What stood out to you in the scripture reading today?

2. Answer at least one of the pondering questions?

3. Personalize the prayer for your own life below:

DAY 15

Scripture Reading: Deuteronomy 24: 1 - 5

Miriam's poem became known by Jewish historians as part of the "Song of the Sea." "Sing ye to the LORD, for He is highly exalted: the horse and his rider hath He thrown into the sea." With timbrel in hand, and dancing with all her heart, Miriam led the women of Israel in their part of the majestic "Song of the Sea." Notice in her song Miriam gave all the credit for the exodus to God. She exalted His name. It was important to her for the women under her leadership to know and understand the power of God. While she could have used many avenues to teach the women, she chose to lead by example, and she chose to lead with singing and dancing. This was truly a joyful time.

Pondering Thoughts:

How do you choose to lead others to Christ? So many times people tend to use negative connotations or fear to impart the need for Christ to others, but looking at Miriam, we can establish there are other ways to lead. What kind of song and dance would you like for God to place on your heart to share with others? What are some of the words you would like to use? Share it... share it today!

Praise and Petitions:

The Eternal God, thank you for the songs and dances we can experience in knowing you. Thank you for each victory shout we can express from our souls. Help me to recognize it is the victory song that causes a nation to have hope. Give me the words to encourage others this day. I ask this in your name, Amen.

Prayer Journaling Notes:

Points from the Editor:

Some of the best encouragement I have received or can offer comes from the reality of what God has done in the past. His promises never to leave us or forsake us are sprinkled into His Word. It always amazes me how God allows our paths to cross with people just at the proper time to hear Him speak to us through them. It should amaze and never surprise. That's our God. You will get to be a part of that encouragement on one side or the other. It's just a matter of time. It's good to know God has ordained it. He knows we often need flesh and blood to provide the conduit for encouragement He alone gives. Why in the world do we think He sent His Son to us, left the Holy Spirit, and promised to bring us to His Kingdom at the appointed time. He is literally dying for fellowship with those created in His image, and we are the blessed ones. The death of His Son is all the proof we need.

Questions and Reflections:

1. What stood out to you in the scripture reading today?

2. Answer at least one of the pondering questions?

3. Personalize the prayer for your own life below:

DAY 16

Scripture Reading: Deuteronomy 24: 6 - 10

Miriam, like all of us, was human. She had faults and failures just like you and me. At one point in her journey, she murmured against her brother. Scriptures tell us she did not like his choice of a wife. It is uncertain who this woman was. Some speculate she was actually Zipporah after she returned to live with Moses in the Wilderness. Some suggest Zipporah had died, and Moses had remarried a woman from Cush or Cushan. Either way, Miriam had voiced her displeasure in Moses' decision. This was a costly mistake for her. But I think the first, and possibly most critical, lesson we should recognize in this story is one of keeping silent when we don't know everything. Silence would have been her friend in this situation. Yet Miriam, like so many of us, decided to speak.

Pondering Thoughts:

Have you ever spoken and wished immediately you could take it back? I have. Think of a time when you did. Why did you have to speak? What was it you said making you regret speaking? How can we refrain from speaking in situations in which God may want us to be quiet?

Praise and Petitions:

The True Vine, thank you for giving us wisdom. My problem with wisdom is I don't always do what I should. I know what I should do, but my flesh causes me much pain. Help me control my voice. I know it is difficult to control our tongues, because James writes of it in your Word. But with your help I can learn to be silent. I ask this in your name, Amen.

Prayer Journaling Notes:

Points from the Editor:

Even fools are thought wise when they remain silent. It's so hard in this world of social media. We can surmise just because others are making their opinions known, we must do so. After all, mine matters as much as anyone's, we reason. Every opinion does not need a voice. Every voice does not need an audience. By not voicing your opinion, do you feel some might think you condone or agree with a different opinion? Do you feel people are counting on you to voice one because you've established yourself as a person with a perpetual opinion. It needs to stop, and that admonition is for me! Yes, I have an opinion. Yes, mine is rooted and grounded in Biblical truth. In my mind it needs to be voiced if no other one is. But my dog is not always in the fight. My opinion, though unspoken many times, should be known though silent by the life I live. For those who are not close enough to know my life, my opinion will not matter anyway. Words spoken cannot ever be stuffed back into the mouth. It's always a grand idea to examine your motive before opening your mouth.

Questions and Reflections:

1. What stood out to you in the scripture reading today?

2. Answer at least one of the pondering questions?

3. Personalize the prayer for your own life below:

DAY 17

Scripture Reading: Deuteronomy 24: 11 - 15

We are not told specifically Miriam was jealous of Moses' wife. But some historians suggest it was in fact jealousy that caused her to speak out. I could see that happening. After all, it was Miriam who saved Moses' life so many years ago. She was the one who had watched over him, and I can only imagine how she felt when he married. But then he had to go marry someone outside of their people. I'm sure that didn't sit well with her at all. But God had a plan for Moses and his wife that Miriam didn't know or understand. As hard as it is for us to believe this, sometimes God just doesn't show us everything. And sometimes, we just don't know what is best for those we love.

Pondering Thoughts:

Who stirs up jealousy in your heart? Be honest. We all have feelings of jealousy. God has feelings of jealousy. The crime is not in the feelings, but in our responses. How have you responded to someone in the past because of a jealous spirit? How do you combat jealousy in your heart today? What advice would you give others to use when dealing with family and jealousy?

Praise and Petitions:

The Truth, I am truly thankful you are a jealous God. I know you are jealous for me, and that makes me feel so special. But I also know jealousy in the wrong way is a bad emotion to entertain in my life. Help me to push wrong feelings of jealousy toward others out of my life. I ask this in your name, Amen.

Prayer Journaling Notes:

Points from the Editor:

We can be jealous - jealous for our families. Jealous for a closer walk with God. Jealous for more... of the Godly things. But we will suffer most when jealousy takes on the face and heart of a great-eyed monster (no offense to all my green-eyed friends). It alters our thoughts and motives. It's an addictive emotion. The more we feed jealousy, the uglier it gets and acts. Whether we see it or not, it's painfully obvious to everyone we know well. Most of the time it just cannot remain silent. And if it can, it scribbles mindless graffiti all over our guilty faces. It stares. It jeers. It sneers. It often even hides behind flattery and empty smiles. It has no place in the life of a believer who has a Deliverer waiting for the monster's head to be surrendered on a platter at His feet. That, my friend, is sweet victory.

Questions and Reflections:

1. What stood out to you in the scripture reading today?

2. Answer at least one of the pondering questions?

3. Personalize the prayer for your own life below:

DAY 18

Scripture Reading: Deuteronomy 24: 16 - 22

The second part of Miriam's sin against Moses involved her questioning his relationship with God. Again, this was another form of jealousy. But to taunt how God spoke to Miriam, Aaron, and Moses pushed things too far. God had to teach Miriam a lesson - a painful lesson in humility. When God gives you a gift, it is never wise to use that gift as leverage or comparisons to others. God equally uses people as He sees fit. I'm sure if Miriam were here today, she would quickly tell us to stay out of God's way when it comes to how He chooses to use others. And we would do well to listen.

Pondering Thoughts:

Have you ever looked at someone and questioned how God was using him/her? It is very tempting to do so, and I have certainly been guilty. It was only God's mercy He didn't judge me immediately. Think of a time when God was way more merciful to you than you were to someone else. What did you learn from that experience? How has it caused you to treat others differently?

Praise and Petitions:

Wonderful, I praise you because your mercies endure forever. You are so much more merciful to me than I deserve. I ask you to help me learn to be merciful to others. I know I need help when it comes to judging how others serve you. Help me work on myself more than others. I ask this in your name, Amen.

Prayer Journaling Notes:

Points from the Editor:

It's none of my business. I am doing my best to just be a vessel God can use. I don't have time or get any good vibes from judgment. When I am tempted to judge, I might: (1) remove myself from regular engagement, or (2) hide posts from my newsfeed. My judgment or reaction to the decisions of others is not pleasing to God. He promises something in His Word about my judgment - I will be judged by the same measure. I can know and am known by the fruit produced from a life. One more promises - mercy always triumphs over judgment! For that I am so thankful. Mercy is what I need most.

Questions and Reflections:

1. What stood out to you in the scripture reading today?

2. Answer at least one of the pondering questions?

3. Personalize the prayer for your own life below:

DAY 19

Scripture Reading: Micah 6: 1 - 5

Miriam learned a valuable lesson because of her jealousy and speaking out against her brother. She learned God doesn't like ugly. God responded to her with swift judgment - seven days of leprosy. Know while God may not strike us down with leprosy, He will not tolerate ugliness in His warrior princesses forever. If we act inappropriately, we can expect His correction. We would do well to remember God cares for all His children, and He will not tolerate us acting unkindly to each other. Judgment begins in His house. We should know better.

Pondering Thoughts:

Think of a time when you were "ugly" and God sent correction. How did you feel during the correcting? We should take great care not to offend others by our words. How can we best protect ourselves from falling into this kind of sin?

Praise and Petitions:

The Word, I thank you for all the instruction you provide to your children. I wish I could say I always do what I am told, but there have been times in my life I was in fact "ugly" towards one of your children. I am sorry. Help me to realize all of your children are precious in your sight, and I should seek to build up. I ask this in your name, Amen.

Prayer Journaling Notes:

Points from the Editor:

When can we rightfully judge a situation or person? We must protect our family, our own personal walk with the Lord, and our relationships. All of them must be fully vetted, and we've covered that in the previous month. I would like to suggest to you every single time I look back and saw a poor judgment, I had a feeling about it in advance. In other words, I should have known better about the circumstance or situation. Instead I moved forward, at least initially. It's made me a different, more self-controlled person. It has made me more guarded, less trusting. My mom always called it a "check in her spirit." And I always hated that phrase, because to my teenage mind it translated into one simple word, "No!" I am so glad she used that modeling for me, because even today I can understand having a reservation on the inside.

Questions and Reflections:

1. What stood out to you in the scripture reading today?

2. Answer at least one of the pondering questions?

3. Personalize the prayer for your own life below:

DAY 20

Scripture Reading: Micah 6: 6 - 10

Why leprosy? This is one of the first questions that comes to my mind when I read about Miriam. Now I am not God, so I may not know the exact answer, but I can conjecture (form my own opinion based on limited information). Leprosy forced a person to live alone, outside the camp, and ostracized from everyone. When Miriam and Aaron spoke against Moses, they ostracized him. They made him feel very alone, without a friend or solace. Perhaps God wanted Miriam to feel what Moses had felt by her actions. Miriam not only spoke against Moses, but also his wife. Perhaps God wanted her to realize how words hurt so deeply. Leprosy allowed of those feelings to become very real to Miriam as she had to stay to herself outside the camp for 7 days.

Pondering Thoughts:

Our actions certainly have consequences. Can you think of a time when your actions alienated you from your family or friends? What happened? What did you learn? How has the experience changed your perspective as you move forward?

Praise and Petitions:

Consolation of Israel, I praise you for your correction even when it is painful. I know there have been times I have hurt someone, and you have responded with discipline. But your discipline is always much more fair than my actions. Help me to remember to treat others as I would want to be treated in all things, even in my words. I ask this in your name, Amen.

Prayer Journaling Notes:

Points from the Editor:

There's a law of nature that eventually proves itself, and does so over and over. We will reap what we sow, more than we sow, and later than we sow. Whether negative or positive consequences, they are coming. Sometimes the consequences are enacted in mysterious ways, but alway humbling ways. Consequences should be feared enough to change our patterns of sowing. The thoughts, the habits, lifestyle - they are all degrees of what we are sowing daily. If we continue practicing sin, it's going to come back to us in multiplied painful ways. It's going to bring personal pain and indirect pain on those we love. The Bible is clear the one who brings trouble on his own household will inherit the wind. Lord, bring discipline to us sooner rather than later.

Questions and Reflections:

1. What stood out to you in the scripture reading today?

2. Answer at least one of the pondering questions?

3. Personalize the prayer for your own life below:

DAY 21

Scripture Reading: Micah 6: 11 - 16

While Miriam wronged Moses, he prayed for her healing. What an incredible lesson in humility! Sometimes when we wrong someone, God uses that person to bless us. Likewise, if someone wrongs us, we should ask God to allow us to bring restoration to him/her. I'm sure this was difficult for Moses as well as Miriam. Yet, what a powerful lesson to both. Forgiveness is such a restoring tool in God's arsenal in the fight against evil. When others wrong you, pray for them. If you wrong someone, pray for forgiveness. Realize who the real enemy of all God's warriors is, and go after the devil unified and in support of one another.

Pondering Thoughts:

Have you ever been wronged, and God used you to help that person? Talk about how you felt when God spoke to you to help him/her. Have you ever wronged someone, and God used that person to help you? How did you feel when he/she reached out a hand of mercy? What lessons have you learned in being hurt or hurting someone else and forgiveness?

Praise and Petitions:

Rabbi, I thank you for all you teach us, especially what you have taught me on forgiveness. I thank you for each time you have sent forgiveness my way. Help me to be able to forgive those who have wronged me as well as ask for forgiveness from those I have wronged. I ask this in your name, Amen.

Prayer Journaling Notes:

Points from the Editor:

Every time, the truth of God's Word flips us on edge. Don't just pray. Pray for your enemies. Don't just forgive those you love. Forgive those who spitefully use you and mean to bring you harm. Can't we get a little solace, a little seething? It feels good at first - it really does. Certainly if God wants vengeance, I can help Him out. No. Nothing good comes from unforgiveness. It's not meant to bring healing to the one who wronged you - it's meant to bring healing to your own crushed bones. Praying for your enemies actually has the power to propel God's outcome - His Will. Who knows, He may be waiting on your sincere prayers to be activated before He can activate your blessing, reconciliation, and wholeness. What's holding you back?

Questions and Reflections:

1. What stood out to you in the scripture reading today?

2. Answer at least one of the pondering questions?

3. Personalize the prayer for your own life below:

DAY 22

Scripture Reading: Psalms 3: 1 - 4

While Miriam waits outside the camp to be healed of leprosy, her people wait for her. The camp does not move until Miriam is healed. This is a testament of how much she was loved. Her people were willing to wait and pray for her healing until she was restored. What a powerful message of restoration! So many times we leave those who are sick behind to fend for themselves, but not Miriam's people. They patiently waiting for God's healing to flood her body. This is a great lesson for us to learn in the Church today. When one of our members is sick, we need to stop and pray for restoration. If we move ahead like nothing is wrong, our brothers or sisters may die in their weakened states. Stop, and pray for healing. Have time for the restoration of your brother or sister.

Pondering Thoughts:

Has someone ever taken the time to stop for you when you were spiritually sick? How did that make you feel? Do you know someone who needs restoration today? What are you doing to help him/her obtain the healing needed for full renewal?

Praise and Petitions:

God, who taketh vengeance, I thank you for fighting for me. I know we should also fight for each other. Help me to pray for healing and restoration for my brothers and sisters who are sick, even if they caused their own sickness. I pray for you to help me be the example for others to follow when someone needs a healing hand. I ask this in your name, Amen.

Prayer Journaling Notes:

Points from the Editor:

We never know when we will be the ones standing in need of healing or restoration of some sort. It's often difficult to know what to say. Do they want me to come see them? Is it a violation of their private pain to just walk in like that? What will I say? Will they see my visit or call as just one more nosey neighbor wanting to get the graphic details and destruction? It's easier when someone is physically sick. When it's not physical, it may be spiritual. It may be mental. Mental sickness like depression, anxiety, or other damaging illnesses and disorders are often hidden from the outside world. Masks are on except at home. Sometimes the disorder is directly correlated to an event or series of events. Sometimes not. The last thing we should do is speculate. If you have never experienced the same private pain, then you cannot understand. Don't try. You can pray, and pray very hard. These disorders are often used by the enemy to wreak havoc. He is, after all, the author of confusion. Why should we expect anything else?

Questions and Reflections:

1. What stood out to you in the scripture reading today?

2. Answer at least one of the pondering questions?

3. Personalize the prayer for your own life below:

DAY 23

Scripture Reading: Psalms 3: 5 - 8

After seven long days, God healed Miriam, and she was restored to the camp. They were able to move forward. I think it is important for us to notice God did require time for her to stop and think about all she had done. There were consequences to her actions. She would go down in Jewish history as the sister who endured leprosy for speaking against her brother. I'm sure this weighed heavily on her mind during her excommunication from her people. But thank God for healing. After God gave her time to think, He healed her. Just because we mess up, and must pay the consequences of our sins, that does not mean we cannot be forgiven and restored. Take courage! If you mess up, take your punishment, but most importantly take your healing!

Pondering Thoughts:

Has the devil ever used a fault of yours to make you think you were no longer valuable to God? How did you rise above this? What steps are you taking now to let God know you are ready to serve again? How can you help others who have fallen return to the warfare, strong as ever?

Praise and Petitions:

Root of David, I praise you for giving me healing. Thank you for allowing me to serve you again even after I fail. Help me to see others may need encouragement from their fall. Guide me as I seek to lend a hand of healing to others. I ask this in your name, Amen.

Prayer Journaling Notes:

Points from the Editor:

We are not finished on Satan.   Not only is he the author of confusion, he's also the accuser of the brethren, and the father of lies.   He tempts us to sin, then taunts us with guilt and condemnation after we do. Miriam had sinned. She deserved death, and we all do. Instead she received what the Bible refers to as severe mercy. She had a miserable seven days and mostly time to think. We need time to think after a season of sinful habits or actions.   We need time to remember God is just and also loving. He is firm, yet also merciful. He disciplines, but is full of grace. Not the grace that is just enough to reach to our sin, but He gives more grace. Abundant grace. Immeasurable grace. Amazing grace. His grace rolls out the red carpet for our return to service, and He knew it all along.

Questions and Reflections:

1. What stood out to you in the scripture reading today?

2. Answer at least one of the pondering questions?

3. Personalize the prayer for your own life below:

DAY 24

Scripture Reading: Ecclesiastes 3: 1 - 5

Miriam's Well is taught in Jewish history as the rock or stone that traveled with Moses and the Israelites. Jewish history teaches the provision of water for the Hebrews came as a direct result of Miriam being with them. How awesome it is to be considered water to a thirsty soul! We should all seek to have the well of living water flowing from our lives so others who are thirsty can have that thirst quenched by our presence. Our lives should be examples to those around us, and they should be able to leave our presence with answers for their lives. No one should feel dry and thirsty because of our testimony. We need to water the people for God.

Pondering Thoughts:

How thirsty do you make people for God? How do you interact with others to give them life water? Who has been a fountain of water for you in your life, and how did that person supply your need for water?

Praise and Petitions:

God, who is rich in mercy, I thank you for the wells of joy you have provided for me. I thank you for each and every time you have sent water my way. Help me to be the well spring for others. Teach me to give sustaining water to your children. I ask this in your name, Amen.

Prayer Journaling Notes:

Points from the Editor:

Miriam's well was full of water. Could it be we all have wells full of something? Are you full of passion splashing out on those around you? Or a love for the Word? Or discernment and wisdom? Or joy? What is your well full of if you had to venture or guess? Or if you know? My well is full of encouragement and a love-passion for the Word of God. I know it because when I give it I often perceive it transferred from me to the person I am with - leaving me full of blessing and them full of exactly what I have imparted in the name of the Lord. At times when I don't know what to say, I walk away so disheartened I was not able to pour into his/her life. It sucks the life out of me when that happens. I have to believe someone else did know what to say.

Questions and Reflections:

1. What stood out to you in the scripture reading today?

2. Answer at least one of the pondering questions?

3. Personalize the prayer for your own life below:

DAY 25

Scripture Reading: Ecclesiastes 3: 6 - 10

For over 120 years, Miriam served her people. Jewish history records her death at around 126 years. We are told she served from the time she was 5 or 6 years old. What a powerful testimony! She remained true to her God and her people for many years. She left behind a legacy of leadership, song, and prophecy. She served with her brothers faithfully, and she is considered as one of the three shepherds of Israel. But like us, there comes a time when our lives are done. Hers was completely full. We should live our lives so when we die, our epitaph can read: She used all she had for God.

Pondering Thoughts:

How do you want to be remembered in life? How long have you served God, and given a natural life span of 70 years, how much time could you have left to do His will? What plans are you making to live your life fuller each day?

Praise and Petitions:

God, who is blessed forever, I thank you for each and every day you give me. I am not worthy of a single day, yet you allow me to breathe. Help me to live my life to the fullest in you. Use all of me for your Kingdom. Help me to work diligently and never waste my precious time on this earth. I ask this in your name, Amen.

Prayer Journaling Notes:

Points from the Editor:

She never retired. She just grew old. She served in whatever way she could all of her days. Not only was her life full, her life was fulfilled. I don't want to waste a single day either. We serve at the capacity we are able to handle. When I had young children, my service was wrapped up at home. I have very little time for any other place of service. I was dead tired every night. My life was devoted to raising up Godly children in an ungodly world without regrets. God was faithful. Now in my service I can do more for others. What's amazing is our children have watched us serve, and I have seen them also follow suit in one way or another. It looks different for each of them. But they are the legacy we live behind - it's inside of them. A gift from parents who sought to do it God's way.

Questions and Reflections:

1. What stood out to you in the scripture reading today?

2. Answer at least one of the pondering questions?

3. Personalize the prayer for your own life below:

DAY 26

Scripture Reading: Ecclesiastes 3: 11 - 15

Miriam, like Moses and Aaron, devoted her whole life to seeing her people free and in their Promised Land. Miriam, like her brothers, did not get to actually make it to the Promised Land on this earth. But that did not deter her from helping her people get as far as they could during her life. So many times we get discouraged because we don't see the "Promised Land" on earth. Yet we should follow Miriam's example and work ever so hard in our churches. They may not double in our lifetime, but they could in the years to come. Don't stop short of the "Promised Land" God has in mind for your family and church. Keep working! Die working! Your family is worth it!

Pondering Thoughts:

Have you ever felt like you would never live to see the fruition of your labor? What are some things you want to see accomplished on earth? How much time do you devote to those things? List some examples of things that have come to pass after someone you know died, but prayed daily for those things to happen. How does this list renew your faith?

Praise and Petitions:

Thou who my soul loveth, I give you honor and glory for everything accomplished on this earth by you. I thank you for all you have done and all you will do. Help me continue to work even if I don't see immediate results. Help my faith in you to grow daily so my loved ones will be saved. I ask this in your name, Amen.

Prayer Journaling Notes:

Points from the Editor:

We don't have the privilege of the full story on our lives. We can't know how it ends or when. We have control, however of what we do every day our feet hit the floor. I remember when my heart was set on fire, and I finally understood. It was clear to me I had wasted so much time living for myself. When I allowed the Spirit of God to make that connection inside of me, all I could think about is how much catching up I had to do. If we are okay with God knowing the end of the story instead of us... if we are okay with any place of service instead of just prominent places of service... if we can handle the menial tasks and the small jobs that don't get much notice by much of anybody... then we are perfect candidates for God to use for His glory alone.

Questions and Reflections:

1. What stood out to you in the scripture reading today?

2. Answer at least one of the pondering questions?

3. Personalize the prayer for your own life below:

DAY 27

Scripture Reading: Ecclesiastes 3: 16 - 22

The water dried up for the Israelites after Miriam's death. We are told in the scriptures the rock simply quit giving them water. Perhaps God was sending them a message it was time to stop wandering and time to move into the Promised Land. There comes a time in our lives when we have to stop depending on water from others and rely on God. Miriam had been a faithful servant of God and a leader for her people, but it was not in her strength Israel existed. We have to remember leaders are sent to us for a time, but our true worship belongs to God.

Pondering Thoughts:

Have you ever put too much faith in a person? Did you get let down? Why do you think we so often depend more on people than on God? What have you learned throughout your walk with God about reliance on Him for all your needs?

Praise and Petitions:

Thou preserver of men, I thank you for every person you have sent my way. I know you had a plan and purpose for their lives, but help me to remember you are the ultimate Friend. You are the savior of your people. Help me to have a proper perspective on how I view leaders in my life. Help me to lead as you would have me lead, but to know when my influence is over. I ask this in your name, Amen.

Prayer Journaling Notes:

Points from the Editor:

You could say God allowed Miriam to leave them high and dry! There are so many lessons in this last part of our time with Miriam. The Promised Land would be an uncomfortable transition - they had wandered long enough to become comfortable doing it while doubting they would ever step foot in it. They had been so dependent on the wonders of God to supply their every need, yet in the Promised Land God wanted to make them the wonder. He had supplied in advance everything they would need and such an abundant variety of fruits and vegetables, milk and honey. But leaving the comforts of then makeshift temporary homes was so difficult. Sometimes God just straight up says, "You're done here. It's over. You stayed here long enough. It's time to move on." He's just so on point with His timing when we have long since stopped feeling it for ourselves. When He takes away your choices, Honey, you are done. And you are in the best hands for where you go next and what you do.

Questions and Reflections:

1. What stood out to you in the scripture reading today?

2. Answer at least one of the pondering questions?

3. Personalize the prayer for your own life below:

DAY 28

Scripture Reading: Ecclesiastes 4: 1 - 5

The whole nation of Israel mourned for their shepherdess... their poetess... their prophetess. Miriam had become and accomplished so much for this nation for at least two generations. She had protected their children, saved their leader, and walked with them through their forty year journey towards the Promised Land. They would not forget her. Their children would talk about her "Song at Sea" and her timbrel dance. Jewish historians would speak of "Miriam's Well" and teach their daughters how important women are to their history. Yes, she would be remembered for her failure, but she would also be remembered for all her successes with the Hebrew journey through the wilderness. Their warrior princess had left them, but her influence would be with them forever.

Pondering Thoughts:

How do you think people will remember you after you are gone? How do you want to be remembered? Name a person who had an impact on your life. Why did that person have such an impact? What do you do to remember him/her?

Praise and Petitions:

The Invincible God, I thank you for the people you have placed in my life. You have always provided a Godly influence for me. There have been many women who have supported and encouraged me. I thank you for every one of them and their testimonies. Help me become the person I need to be to encourage others. I ask this in your name, Amen.

Prayer Journaling Notes:

Points from the Editor:

My Mother was my Godly influence. I'll never forget being asked a few years ago if I remember her. My response was something like this: Are you kidding me!? Yes! I remember her every time I don't set the table. I remember her every time I pray for someone who desperately needs it - with the person - on the spot - no matter where we are... Walmart... Ball game... Phone call... Text message... I remember her every time I crack open my Bible and Sunday school lesson to study before teaching. I remember her every time it dawns on me my daughter will soon be the age I was when I lost her. I remember her every time I fight for my family, sacrifice something to make arrangements for their needs. And every time I notice my worn out panties have been washed, folded, and put up again instead of being thrown away, I remember my Mother. You will leave behind that which you have become for those who love you most. It will happen.

Questions and Reflections:

1. What stood out to you in the scripture reading today?

2. Answer at least one of the pondering questions?

3. Personalize the prayer for your own life below:

DAY 29

Scripture Reading: Ecclesiastes 4: 6 - 10

Miriam left her mark. She had her personal testimony. Her story lives on through the ages. Her victories can be remembered; her defeats can be critiqued. But what about our stories? What are we leaving behind for others to follow? I know this isn't the questioning section, but think about your life for a moment as I think about mine. God has given us this enormous responsibility to be both an heir and a warrior in His Kingdom. He sends us resources and talents to use. He provides training for the warfare in which we will engage. We need to remember our history, just like Miriam's history, is written each day of our lives. I don't know about you, but as for me, I want there to be more victories than defeats. It's time to go to battle and fight with all my might.

Pondering Thoughts:

Do you feel like you live a life of victory in Christ, or does it seem like you have far more setbacks than you have victories? What causes most of your setbacks? How have you prayed for deliverance from those setbacks? What is your battle plan for moving forward?

Praise and Petitions:

Rock of my refuge, I thank you for helping me with each victory in my life. I know you protect your children, and I feel your protection when the enemy seems to advance in his tactics to destroy me. I pray for peace in the battle and protection for me and my family. I pray for your divine intervention when I would lose within my own strength. I ask this in your name, Amen.

Prayer Journaling Notes:

Points from the Editor:

The reality is this: there is no victory without war, a battle, a conflict between two opposing sides. When life is never difficult, there are no victories to stake and claim. But when there is a conflict, arise my dear sister, and be ready to fight for your personal victory, your family's victory. In every victory, God is preparing a glorious testimony. You may not be able to see it now. Sometimes they take years, and other times only days. God fights for you and with you. Don't lay down, child of God. Don't you dare give up! He's asking you a question in the midst of every battle. He's asking, "What do you want?" If you want His will and you want victory in the name of Jesus, then you can be assured it will come. It may not be in your time, but it will always be in His time and grand plan.

Questions and Reflections:

1. What stood out to you in the scripture reading today?

2. Answer at least one of the pondering questions?

3. Personalize the prayer for your own life below:

DAY 30

Scripture Reading: Ecclesiastes 4: 11 - 16

My Song of the Sea
sbo

My enemy thought he had me surrounded.
He thought he had me dead to rights.
But what he failed to realize in his haste,
I had turned my battle over to Jesus during the night.

Though Satan sent waves around me crashing,
And he thought I'd drown in defeat,
He forgot my Captain walks on water,
With Jesus there is no need for retreat.

My adversary looks a little weary.
He looks as though he's backing away.
I'm sure he'll come back with a vengeance,
But with renewed faith I'll live to fight another day.

Pondering Thoughts:

What's your song of the sea? Write it! Share it! Live it!

Praise and Petitions:

The Lamb, I thank you for fighting with me in all my battles. I praise you for the victory you bring to each fight. Help me to stand strong against the advances of our enemy. Help me fight the good fight! I ask this in your name, Amen.

Prayer Journaling Notes:

Points from the Editor:

According to Ezekiel 28, it's clear we have a formidable foe on our hands. Not to frighten you, but he's way more intelligent than any of us. Whatever your IQ, he has a higher one. He's talented, wealthy, and beautiful. You have not met your match, but he's way more weightier opponent than any of us could imagine. As a matter of fact, he's a being God created in complete perfection. It just turned sour when he wanted the glory for everything he was. And if you are walking devotedly with God, he's (pardon the expression please) madder than Hades at you because he's running out of time. But just hold on and take a look at your God. He's not the opposite and opposing force of evil. He cannot be compared to any force, created or man-made. He is God alone, and there is no one like Him. Satan has been outmatched, and he knows it. When the Mighty Warrior steps onto the scene, it's just a matter of time, and the victory is His. That's our God. What an awesome last day for the life of Miriam - What a warrior princess!

Questions and Reflections:

1. What stood out to you in the scripture reading today?

2. Answer at least one of the pondering questions?

3. Personalize the prayer for your own life below:

July
Ruth - The Follower

Scripture Reading - Verses about Ruth's life as well as scriptures from the Book of Hosea

I love the story of Ruth. She had tragic grief early in her life, but God allowed her to have a greater love story.   She lost much; but she gained even more. God sent her handfuls of purpose in her life. He empowered her with a love that started something truly amazing for Israel. She would become the great-grandmother of David. Ruth's devotion to her mother-in-law allows us to see what a true warrior princess she was. She gave her life to her husband's family. She, though a foreigner, became one of them so her family could have a heritage.

No one knows how long it took Ruth to fall in love with Boaz. Perhaps it was instant; maybe it took some time.   But I love the fact she was willing to do anything for the memory of her husband and to bring joy back to her mother-in-law's heart. What exuberant expectancy must have flowed from the heart of Ruth when she knew she was carrying a child, the child of Boaz who would father the greatest king ever known to Israel. My, how God works! Join me as we dive into Ruth's story - an amazing love story for a great warrior princess.

DAY 1

Scripture Reading: Ruth 2: 1 - 5

Even though Ruth came from the land of Moab, full of incestuous idolatry, her name means "friend of God." As we look closely at her life, we will find she was truly a friend. She was the kind of friend you can't easily offend. In a lifetime if you have one friend like Ruth, you are very rich. Many friends come and go, but one like Ruth will stick with you until the day you die. In her story God proves to us once again it doesn't matter as much from where we have come, but rather how we act. What an honor to be called a "friend of God!" Allies are important in this battle against evil. We should seek to align ourselves with God as well as friends of God.

Pondering Thoughts:

If you had to think of one word to describe your best friend, what would that word be? How do you think your friend(s) view you? What word(s) would be used to describe you?   What are some characteristics of a true friend?

Praise and Petitions:

Chief Cornerstone, I thank you for your friendship. You are a much better friend than I am. I wish I would never displease you. It is not possible for you to disappoint, because you are perfect. Help me be a better friend to you as well as to others. I want to be a worthy friend. I ask this in your name, Amen.

Prayer Journaling Notes:

Points from the Editor:

It's through the story of Ruth I think we learn how to be a lady of love, a lady of family, a lady of resourcefulness, a lady of wisdom, and a love for God's plan despite what others around might feel is best. It seemed her culture, her mother-in-law, and perhaps others felt she needed to have a different strategy than what she actually used. I can't wait to see what I learn in this warrior princess named at birth "friend of God."

Questions and Reflections:

1. What stood out to you in the scripture reading today?

2. Answer at least one of the pondering questions?

3. Personalize the prayer for your own life below:

DAY 2

Scripture Reading: Ruth 2: 6 - 10

Ruth was living in Moab; she was just a young girl when Mahlon came from Bethlehem and married her. We cannot be certain how long they were married, but according to the Scriptures, Mahlon was in Moab about ten years. Then he died. Mahlon came to Moab to escape famine, and while he was there he met and married Ruth. It is unlikely Ruth knew God before her marriage to Mahlon, and for some reason God did not allow them to have children. She was barren, or Mahlon was sterile. Either way, their marriage was fruitless. Ruth bore this barrenness sorely because she knew how much it pained Naomi. Yet, she was faithful. There are times in our lives when we feel like we are in a barren state. It would be easy to bail out and find a better situation in life, but God may call us to stay in this infertile situation for His plan to be fulfilled in our lives. Remain faithful even in barrenness.

Pondering Thoughts:

Can you recall a time in your life when you felt utterly barren in spirit? What are some of the thoughts that ran through your mind at that time? How were you able to become fruitful? What would be your advice to someone who is experiencing barrenness in her life today?

Praise and Petitions:

Deliverer, I thank you for the times in my life when I don't feel fruitful, but yet you love me. I know we are supposed to always bear fruit, but I know we can find ourselves in Moab. Help me to remember where you want me to be in order to be productive for the Kingdom. I ask this in your name, Amen.

Prayer Journaling Notes:

Points from the Editor:

Whether you face infertility in child-bearing or in fruit bearing for the Kingdom, it's a hard place to be. It's hard to trust God month-after-month when you see no positive results. Dreams are deferred. Stories are stalled. Hope is surely half-hearted. But make no mistake, God knew what you would experience during every day of barrenness. He knows your longings, and He longs too. He longs to give you the desires of your heart, whether physically or spiritually. But He procrastinates for a purpose. He is avoiding some action that really needs to be accomplished. He seemingly does less urgent things first while He puts off actions that are more urgent. It's almost like He is waiting until the last minute to bring to you that thing for which you long. And it's true, He likes to work when nothing else will. It's the perfect backdrop for Him to increase our faith, strengthen us, and display His glory. Just hold on. Wait.

Questions and Reflections:

1. What stood out to you in the scripture reading today?

2. Answer at least one of the pondering questions?

3. Personalize the prayer for your own life below:

DAY 3

Scripture Reading: Ruth 2: 11-15

Ruth married Mahlon, but yet his name meant "the sickly one." It is likely he was in ill health when they married. Yet we have no indication Ruth ever complained or wished she had married another. Rather, the only evidence of Ruth we can find is extreme loyalty. You may feel like you have relationships with others who are sickly, whether physically, spiritually, or emotionally. Your personal fulfillment may not be met by those who are sick, but yet, you remain loyal. God honors loyalty. You may never have fulfillment in that particular relationship, and you may always be the nurse, or caregiver. Do not lose heart. God rewards the loyal. He hears the cry of the faithful. Loyalty is a trait carried by a warrior princess.

Pondering Thoughts:

Do you consider loyalty to be a priority in your life? Think back to a time when you showed loyalty but did not receive fulfillment in your own life. How did this make you feel? Where do you gain strength to remain in relationships where it is your loyalty keeping you in them?

Praise and Petitions:

Gracious and Merciful God, I praise you for your loyalty to your people. Your word is always just and true. I want to be the kind of friend people can count as loyal, and I want to be loyal to you. Help me to make the right decisions in life and prove to be a forever friend. I ask this in your name, Amen.

Prayer Journaling Notes:

Points from the Editor:

To be loyal is to show complete and constant support for someone or something. The most loyal breeds of dogs are God's gift to use in a true picture of loyalty. Loyal breeds: (a) sit by the side of their owner each day; (b) save others from harm's way; (c) defend their owner's home; (d) protect those who fight along side of them; (e) risk their own lives for your safety (Resource: iheartdogs.com, Kristina Lotz, 2014). When we are loyal, we are willing to do these things - defend, fight, protect, sacrifice, and even just sit by the side of the object of our loyalty. It's never wasted time, wasted energy. He promises never to leave us or forsake us. At times, we move away from Him. We distance ourselves. Others may leave you, and that's their decision. Yours is a character of true loyalty.

Questions and Reflections:

1. What stood out to you in the scripture reading today?

2. Answer at least one of the pondering questions?

3. Personalize the prayer for your own life below:

DAY 4

Scripture Reading: Ruth 2: 16 - 23

Naomi lost her husband and both sons in Moab, and she was ready to go home to Bethlehem. So, she told her daughter-in-laws "goodbye," but they wanted to go with her. Both Orpah and Ruth traveled with her for a while, but Naomi insisted they return to their homeland. She knew she would never have sons for them to marry. Orpah decided she would go back. But Ruth refused. Ruth knew Naomi needed her, and she also knew the Lord was blessing Israel. Ruth decided she wanted to leave Moab forever, even if it meant she would never remarry. She was ready to sacrifice all so she might live with God's people. She wanted to serve Naomi's God. So many times people decide to live in a spiritual Moab because it looks more promising than the spiritual Israel in life.

Pondering Thoughts:

Why do you think people, like Orpah, choose to stay in Moab rather than to travel to Israel (metaphorically speaking)? God's blessing is in Israel. His bread is in Israel. What has been your experience in Moab? In Israel? (metaphorically)

Praise and Petitions:

Immanuel, I thank you for your blessings. I thank you for the Promised Land of Heavenly Benefits. Help me to keep the Promised Land in focus as I live my life. I don't want to find myself pining away in Moab because things looked better there for a moment. I ask this in your name, Amen.

Prayer Journaling Notes:

Points from the Editor:

It's comfortable there. It's known. There's little risk in just staying where you are. You might be miserable, and you are not sure whether you'll be happier making a badly needed change. What if it's a huge mistake? You deliberate the thoughts for years sometimes. Then looking back with regrets, we often say, "I should have... could have... would have..." Decide. Make up your mind, even with all the interjections from well-meaning individuals. It's what Ruth did. She determined in her heart what she would do. Nothing, nor not a single soul was stopping her. She was set, not double minded. That's an example of a made-up mind!

Questions and Reflections:

1. What stood out to you in the scripture reading today?

2. Answer at least one of the pondering questions?

3. Personalize the prayer for your own life below:

DAY 5

Scripture Reading: Ruth 3: 1 - 5

Ruth told her mother-in-law Ruth was not going to go back to Moab. She decided she wanted to go with Naomi, and only death could separate them. This is a phenomenal act of love and devotion. Ruth could have blamed Naomi for her condition, but rather she chose to bear Naomi's deepest sorrow with her. There is such a powerful message in this story. So many times we, as women, see ourselves becoming blamers and bitter women at circumstances in our lives. But not Ruth. She chose to be an encourager even in her discouragement. Ruth had something in her character that shouted, "I'm not just your friend; I'm your friend for LIFE until death takes me." That is a powerful friend!

Pondering Thoughts:

Who is the Ruth in your life? How does this friend prove her love for you? For whom do you play the role of Ruth? How do you encourage your friends?

Praise and Petitions:

King of Glory, I thank you for every Ruth in my life. We live in a harsh world, and we need friends who will stick with us until death. Help me be a Ruth in someone's life. Show me how I can help bear the burdens and sorrows of a friend. I ask this in your name, Amen.

Prayer Journaling Notes:

Points from the Editor:

Ruth's hardship could have caused her to take on the wrong V-word. She could have seen herself as a victim. Instead, she became a victor - quite a fitting description for a warrior princess, don't you think? No doubt she had every reason to feel victimized. How unfair to lose a husband so early in their union! The most powerful personal decision we can make about our circumstances is to focus on others versus ourselves. Isaiah 58 tells us where our healing will come from in the midst of personal pain. When we work to loosen chains of injustice, share our food with the hungry, provide the poor with shelter, clothe the naked, and not turn away our own flesh and blood, the most amazing thing happens. We will look up and notice light has broken forth, and our healing has come quickly. Our righteous acts go before us, and the glory of the Lord follows closely behind. And we have been victorious!

Questions and Reflections:

1. What stood out to you in the scripture reading today?

2. Answer at least one of the pondering questions?

3. Personalize the prayer for your own life below:

DAY 6

Scripture Reading: Ruth 3: 6 - 10

Let's take a moment to look at a comparison between Orpah and Ruth. First of all, Orpah's decision did not make her a bad daughter-in-law or friend. She traveled with Ruth at least part of the way to Bethlehem. But at some point Orpah realized she couldn't help Naomi, and so she parted ways. Ruth, however, could not bear the thought of leaving her mother-in-law, and she stayed close. There is no way humanly possible you can be a Ruth to every friend. You do not have the stamina to meet the emotional needs of all the friends in your life, and there are times when you will need a Ruth in your own life. So before we quickly judge Orpah, let us ponder the possibility she simply could not meet Naomi's needs. Maybe she was younger and needed someone to care for her. Perhaps she was already drained from having lived with Naomi's bitterness for ten years or more. She could have been in depression from her own loss. Just because God may use you or me as a Ruth in someone's life doesn't prove we are in any way more spiritual or needed than the Orpahs in life. It's really all about God's timing. If you feel more like an Orpah today, don't be discouraged in that status. Your day to be a Ruth will come.

Pondering Thoughts:

How many times have you felt like Orpah rather than Ruth? What did you learn during those times? How can we best prepare to be a Ruth for the Naomis in our lives?

Praise and Petitions:

Jesus Christ the Righteous, I praise you for all you are to me. Help me to see the benefit of being both Orpah and Ruth in the relationships you provide for me in my life. I ask this in your name, Amen.

Prayer Journaling Notes:

Points from the Editor:

If God doesn't call you to be a Ruth, then it's simply a blessing for someone else. Conversely, if you find yourself in a Ruth role, you will not wonder. It will not be a burden. You will know it's your place. you will treasure it forever. Practically speaking, in a life where many women work outside the home, I am convinced many times the position of Ruth has to be filled by more than one person. And gladly so. When a sister is in a great need, whether family or not, it's a near impossible task to meet all the needs all the time. So release yourself from any guilt or condemnation you feel when you cannot be a Ruth as badly as you desire to be. Release yourself from judging Orpah; you may play her role one day. It may not be because you want to, but because you have to do so.

Questions and Reflections:

1. What stood out to you in the scripture reading today?

2. Answer at least one of the pondering questions?

3. Personalize the prayer for your own life below:

DAY 7

Scripture Reading: Ruth 3: 11 - 15

Walking away from Moab could not have been an easy thing for Ruth. Everyone she knew and loved had been in Moab. Her husband's grave was in Moab. Yet when God called, she packed up and started her journey. There will be times in our lives when God calls us out of Moab. It may not be an easy thing to leave, but if we can just trust Him, we will find the good in Israel. So many times we get comfortable where we are, and it becomes necessary for God to move us in order to use us. Think of all Ruth would have missed had she remained in Moab. She would have likely never become the ancestress to our Lord and Savior, Jesus Christ. What an honor she had because she obeyed!

Pondering Thoughts:

How difficult is it for you to look past what you have to what you could have? What have you given up in order to enjoy what God had planned for an area of your life? How did you deal with walking away?

Praise and Petitions:

Majesty on High, I thank you for helping me walk away from things I loved in this life when you knew I had a better path to follow. It is never easy to do this, and I pray for your strength in the future when you direct me in a path unknown to me. I pray I can always follow you and be unafraid, but I know I cannot do this without your help. I ask this in your name, Amen.

Prayer Journaling Notes:

Points from the Editor:

Learning is hard. Goodbye is a necessary life skill. Dr. Seuss is quoted, "Don't cry because it's over. Smile because it happened." Goodbyes are only hard because of the good memories that flood the mind in the leaving. It's fuller than it would have been otherwise. The goodbye is now added to that chapter of life like a closing paragraph. Take a deep breath and understand transitions, goodbyes, and closures are part of life. God ordains them when we aren't ready. He ordains them in mysterious ways because He alone knows we are really never ready for them, even if we talk a good talk. If we were, we'd have already made them happen ourselves. I thank my God who knows best; He holds my transitions in His safe hands.

Questions and Reflections:

1. What stood out to you in the scripture reading today?

2. Answer at least one of the pondering questions?

3. Personalize the prayer for your own life below:

DAY 8

Scripture Reading: Ruth 3: 16 - 18

Have you ever been in a foreign country? Have you ever felt like you were the odd person in the room? I'm sure Ruth had no idea just how different her life would become when she left with Naomi, but she was about to get a lesson in being the odd person in the room. Yes, there are times God places us in uncomfortable settings. It may seem like all eyes are on us. When we speak our accent gives us away; we are foreigners. We may not know when we arrive what God plans to do with us, but we can be certain He doesn't place us in foreign lands for no reason. Hold on, and God will reveal to you the plan. Stay calm and learn the language as quickly as you can.

Pondering Thoughts:

Think back to a time when you felt like a foreigner. What was God doing in your life? How did you respond? What did you learn from the experience? There are many lessons we can learn in a foreign land, but the most important one would be what God is doing in our lives.

Praise and Petitions:

Only Begotten Son of God, I thank you for taking me into new territories where I can learn more from you. While I don't always like to be out of my comfort zone, I know there is much work to be done, and it can't always be done right at home. Help me to be willing to go on adventures and into foreign places when you think I should. Help me to be brave and always represent my Father. I ask this in your name, Amen.

Prayer Journaling Notes:

Points from the Editor:

The closer we get to God, the more foreign the culture in which we live becomes. God never meant for us to get comfortable here. He set eternity in our hearts so we would long for it. He clearly tells us in scripture to occupy ourselves until His return. In a classroom of planet earth, the Master Teacher says, "Get busy!" We've got work to do that matters here for now, and there for later - not just work though. What's His work for you to do? Where's your sweet spot? What do you most love to do as you occupy until the return of your Lord? It's been said there are at least three clues that can lead you to the answer. When I'm in my sweet spot: (a) I am energized by doing that thing. (b) People love to watch me do that thing. (c) I get better and better at doing that thing. Stop wasting time that was never yours to waste. Every day is a gift to give back to the Giver.

Questions and Reflections:

1. What stood out to you in the scripture reading today?

2. Answer at least one of the pondering questions?

3. Personalize the prayer for your own life below:

DAY 9

Scripture Reading: Ruth 4: 1 - 5

Ruth was not raised as a Jew. She was a Moabite. Her people had served many gods, and she was accustomed to idol worship. While this likely left her empty and void, to embrace the God of the Israelites must have been frightening for her. We know she was likely married for Mahlon for about ten years, and during this time she must have seen something in this Jewish family that made her want to convert. She made a decision to change her way of life forever. We all face situations in our lives where we have decisions of this magnitude to make. God calls us to leave our familiar to embark on a journey of unfamiliar territory. We have to learn new ways; we have to change our way of thinking. It is not an easy journey, but a necessary one to please Him.

Pondering Thoughts:

Has God ever called you to change who you were? How did it happen? What struggles did you face as you went through the metamorphous of change? What did you learn about yourself and God during the transition?

Praise and Petitions:

Redeemer, I praise you because you have provided me with a plan for my life. In this plan, I know there will likely be many changes, and while that frightens me, I know they are only there to help me become a better Christian. I ask for you to help me follow your leading and do what is necessary to be a fruitful warrior princess for you. I ask this in your name, Amen.

Prayer Journaling Notes:

Points from the Editor:

Sometimes it's radical, sometimes gradual. But it's coming. Change is part of this life, and thank goodness it is. It could not be more refreshing at times. We can totally underestimate how difficult it would be at other times. But it's a muscle-making move on the part of a very intentional Master. He never intends to leave us where we are. He's calling us to step it up, to wake up. He's not about our comfort zone. He knows when change won't completely devastate us. He knows when it seems to be long over due, at least in our eyes. He knows, too, when we are ready. "See, I am doing a new thing! Now it springs up; do you not perceive it? I am making a way in the wilderness and streams in the wasteland." Isaiah 43:19 (NIV) If we could only see with radical or even gradual change comes miracles like this, we'd stand to our feet, change out of our favorite jammies and slippers, and step right out into it.

Questions and Reflections:

1. What stood out to you in the scripture reading today?

2. Answer at least one of the pondering questions?

3. Personalize the prayer for your own life below:

DAY 10

Scripture Reading: Ruth 4: 6 - 10

Ruth and Naomi returned to Bethlehem during the harvest of the barley. Now why do you think that was significant? Significant enough to have special attention brought to this fact in Scripture? Barley represents souls for the Christian. The more you harvest, the more souls you have claimed for the Kingdom. It is significant God chose this time, the beginning of the barley harvest, to bring Naomi and Ruth home. It is through Ruth's seed the Messiah would come to earth as a fresh new seed from the bowels of antiquity, from the Ancient of Days. Do you recognize the significance of this? Talk about a barley harvest! This also signifies we should not question or doubt when God does things. He has a plan, and when His timing is right, He'll send us where He wants us to be. The barley harvest signifies God wants us to be fruitful in our efforts. He sends us in the beginning of the harvest so we can glean as much as possible from His benefits. I don't know about you, but I sure could use a barley harvest in my life.

Pondering Thoughts:

Have you ever had a barley harvest in your life? What happened? How did you reap the bounty? What did you learn during this time of gathering in the grain? How did you share it with others?

Praise and Petitions:

Strength of Israel, I thank you for the barley harvests you have sent in my life. We are so swift to give emphasis to the famines in our lives, but we often forget to testify of God's glory in the harvests. Thank you! Help me to remember every time you have moved for me and sent me fruit. I ask this in your name, Amen.

Prayer Journaling Notes:

Points from the Editor:

Most of the time there's more drama in the famine. We find in our conversations people will often relate more to the famine, less to the harvest. It's shock and awe content. But the harvest can be more like sensationalism - is it really true God was that good to you? Really, because I cannot imaging He would ever be that good to me. The harvest is often discomfited. Even Joseph did a terrible job disclosing to his brothers there was a harvest coming. It can seem like self-serving conversation, like He's in my world more than He is in your life. We have to be carefully and completely humble as we give God glory for the harvests. A harvest never comes without toil, labor, planting, pruning, weeding, and fertilizing. There's work, the spiritual kind. But there's great reward, multiplied, pressed down, and overflowing. After all, that is the law of the harvest, and it never fails to be true.

Questions and Reflections:

1. What stood out to you in the scripture reading today?

2. Answer at least one of the pondering questions?

3. Personalize the prayer for your own life below:

DAY 11

Scripture Reading: Ruth 4: 11 - 15

Naomi had a wealthy kinsmen by the name of Boaz, and Ruth learned he had barley fields that needed to be harvested. So Ruth requested to go and gather barley for Naomi and her so they could have their needs supplied. This is so enlightening to me. She immediately found a way to be helpful as soon as they got back to Bethlehem. She did not request time to rest and adjust to her new life. She immediately threw herself into work. She wanted to be profitable to Naomi. Ruth was aware of their needs, and Esther knew she had the ability to help. That is the spirit of a warrior princess. "Show me what needs to be done, and let me do it." That's the attitude to have in order to see mountains moved in our lives. She could have easily been justified to have pined away, like Naomi was doing, but rather she chose to encourage herself, and as a result, she brought life back to Naomi.

Pondering Thoughts:

Do you like bringing life back to people? Have you ever faced a similar situation where this needed to happen? What did you do? How do you identify with Ruth in this setting? How do you look for ways to bring life back to others?

Praise and Petitions:

Consuming Fire, thank you for every opportunity you send my way to work for your Kingdom. Help me to take advantage of the moments you place in our lives to be useful. Lead me to the fields of barley where you want me to glean. I ask this in your name, Amen.

Prayer Journaling Notes:

Points from the Editor:

In our community fundraisers are huge. Prayer circles are pretty amazing too. Let's not wait until a funeral to show up with food. I will never forget the love we experienced from my community after the loss of both my parents when none of us children were over 27 years of age. They came in droves from everywhere - people I barely knew brought more food than four of us could have eaten in a week's time. It's what we do, especially when we don't know what else to do. The comfort of the crowd gathered around us meant more than the comfort food in their dishes. Some dishes we never returned because we had no idea whose they were! When someone is in need, be a part of meeting that need. Get busy. Bake a cake that can be part of the fundraising plates. Drop off a case of drinks. Order a plate. What can you do? Help organize a prayer circle. Don't reason out whether the person is going to be healed or is too close to inevitable demise. That's not your place. A prayer circle can do more good for a weary and discouraged family than we'll ever be able to imagine. One thing they will know if their loved one passes, it won't be because people failed to pray. "Do not withhold good from those to whom it is due, when it is in your power to act." Proverbs 3:27 (NIV)

Questions and Reflections:

1. What stood out to you in the scripture reading today?

2. Answer at least one of the pondering questions?

3. Personalize the prayer for your own life below:

DAY 12

Scripture Reading: Ruth 4: 16 - 22

Ruth knew Boaz's position in Bethlehem, and she knew she needed to find grace in his eyes. Her survival in a foreign land would depend on it. Dear friend, while you are called to be a warrior, you are also called to be a princess. There comes a time in your life when you need to put a hold on fighting and look for the opportunities to find favor. Not every person you encounter is an enemy. Some are allies. We need favor with those around us. We should never think we don't need the grace of others. Ruth realized what a blessing it would be for her, and how much more she could help Naomi, if she had a benefactor like Boaz. Look for those around you who can help you and find grace in their eyes. Remember, all we do is for the Kingdom!

Pondering Thoughts:

Who has been a Boaz in your life? How did you find favor with him/her? What did you do to find grace in his/her eyes? How did it help you do more for the Kingdom of God?

Praise and Petitions:

Great Shepherd of the Sheep, I praise you for all you have done in my life. I thank you for the people you have sent my way who have given me grace. Help me to be the person I need to be to help others in your Kingdom. Let me be a female Boaz or Ruth when you need me to be one. I ask this in your name, Amen.

Prayer Journaling Notes:

Points from the Editor:

It's hard to trust. Who is my friend? Who might be sending me kisses, but in reality they are an enemy? We need wisdom and discernment in the worst way. We are vulnerable when we are needy. It's best not to look for a friend or favor when you are at risk for giving in to what really feels like support. If they were not there in your life before, they might not have pure motives now. With that said, God is the resource for every provision of favor. He has the uncanny ability to either point His child in the direction of favor or straight up bring favor to your front door. I've seen it firsthand. It will happen. It's at that moment we want to rebuke the enemy and our own self-talk when every doubt floods our weary minds. Don't look a gift horse in the mouth (finding fault with a gift). Take it. Claim it, and let favor change your situation for God's glory.

Questions and Reflections:

1. What stood out to you in the scripture reading today?

2. Answer at least one of the pondering questions?

3. Personalize the prayer for your own life below:

DAY 13

Scripture Reading: Hosea 1: 1 - 5

The Bible tells us Ruth "hap" (KJV) or happened by chance to be in the part of the field where Boaz was going to be. Don't you just love it when things just "happen." Like out of the blue, God just moves in a mighty way for you. You should never feel like you have to do everything in this battle. God sends you blessings along the way. There are times when He directly intervenes for you, and you should rejoice when those times come. Give Him thanks when He sends them, and then glean your heart away at these newfound blessings. He knows when to send you a Boaz, and He knows how to send you to the right barley field right on time.

Pondering Thoughts:

Have you ever just "happened" to be at the right place at the right time to receive a huge blessing from God? Reminisce when that happened for you. How did you receive it? How did this build your faith in God? What would you tell someone who desperately needs a supernatural event in a barley field of life?

Praise and Petitions:

Judge of all the Earth, I thank you for every blessing you have sent my way, even when I didn't expect them. Sometimes I think those are the best kind. Help me to look for the unexpected from you, and help me to use what you send for your Kingdom. I ask this in your name, Amen.

Prayer Journaling Notes:

Points from the Editor:

I love this quote from an unknown author: "Opportunity dances with those already on the dance floor." Sweet princess, you have got to get yourself out there. It's what Ruth did. She wasted no time, and her Boaz was captivated. She wasn't really looking for him; she was looking for barley. He picked her out. He arranged for more barley to be left behind on purpose. Ruth wasn't the only one who found favor on that day. "He who finds a wife finds a good thing and obtains favor from the Lord." Proverbs 18:22 (NIV) You must watch, when God pours His favor out on you, it's almost always a set up centered on a much larger purpose and strategy. The favor wasn't just meant for you, but others as well - spiritually, financially, physically, and sometimes in multiples. It's just the nature of our God to work all things for the good of those who love Him and are called according to His purposes. If you haven't seen it happen in your life yet, trust you will.

Questions and Reflections:

1. What stood out to you in the scripture reading today?

2. Answer at least one of the pondering questions?

3. Personalize the prayer for your own life below:

DAY 14

Scripture Reading: Hosea 1: 6 - 11

When Boaz came in from Bethlehem, he noticed Ruth, and he inquired who she was. His reapers told Boaz she was the Moabite who came with Naomi, and she had asked to glean. They also told him she had been there all day, except for one little break. This tells me Ruth went there with a mission, and she wasn't there to play. She was a hard working woman. Warrior Princesses do not shirk from duty, and they work hard. We cannot get what we need to get accomplished taking breaks and naps all day. If we want to reach this world for Christ and reap personal benefits for our family, we have to be willing to work long and hard. Recently I was up until about 2AM talking with someone who needed encouragement and God's help. I felt like it was my calling even though I had a full day of work ahead. There are times we have to just buckle down and remember rest will come.

Pondering Thoughts:

Do you find it difficult to complete tasks? How do you approach difficult jobs? What do you think others, like a Boaz, would notice about you? How do you manage your time? Personal, professional, and spiritual?

Praise and Petitions:

My High Tower, I thank you for the tasks I am given to do for the Kingdom, and I want to always do the kind of work you are pleased for me to do. I know there may be times when I want to take a break, and I'm weary. But I ask for strength to continue in your harvest. I ask this in your name, Amen.

Prayer Journaling Notes:

Points from the Editor:

Breaks and rest are more satisfying after hard work. They are certainly more deserved, but there is nothing like rest after just a few hours of raking pine straw. Or a week of working on a difficult project. You rest with a feeling of accomplishment. What we really need after a satisfying meal is a walk, not a nap! But our body craves what it does not necessarily need! I heard a statement recently and my unsuccessful search for an author turned up no answer - the most miserable soul is the one with unfulfilled responsibility. "A little sleep, a little slumber, a little folding of the hands to rest - and poverty will come on you like a thief and scarcity like an armed man." Proverbs 24:33-34 (NIV) Our bodies were meant to be busy. Our 660+ muscles will only strengthen when stretched. You have inside of you immeasurable power and energy to do the very things that will bring fulfillment to your soul. Then, your rest will be so sweet, your burdens lighter the next day, and your energy multiplied.

Questions and Reflections:

1. What stood out to you in the scripture reading today?

2. Answer at least one of the pondering questions?

3. Personalize the prayer for your own life below:

DAY 15

Scripture Reading: Hosea 2: 1 - 5

Boaz wanted to provide for Ruth and Naomi, so he instructed Ruth to glean only from his fields. He wanted her protected, so he also told her to stay close to his maidens. Girls, do we not all want a Boaz in our lives! Here's the thing, while we may in fact have an earthly Boaz (as I feel I do), it is even more important to have a spiritual Boaz in our lives. God is so gracious to each of us, and He longs to protect us in His fields. We just have to stop wandering off like grazing cattle into fields that look greener to us. God has a plan for each of our lives, and we would do well to remember this as we wake up each morning and go into the barley fields.

Pondering Thoughts:

What do you look for in a Boaz? How has God been a spiritual Boaz for you in your life? What do you gain from gleaning in His fields? How does His protection make you feel like you are a very special Ruth?

Praise and Petitions:

The Eternal God, thank you for being the spiritual Boaz in my life. Thank you for helping me see where I need to be and keeping me safe. Help me to stay focused in the barley field of life where you want me. Don't let me wander in the wrong field. I ask this in your name, Amen.

Prayer Journaling Notes:

Points from the Editor:

No one else we put on a pedestal reserved only for our true Kinsman Redeemer will ever make the cut. Though He doesn't demand we place Him there, He certainly commands that we do. Untold promises are attached to use when the One who sits enthroned upon our hearts is given rightful dominion there. Don't let someone else sit there. Don't set him/her up to fail you. It's not fair to an imperfect soul to wish he/she will be for you who only the True Kinsman Redeemer can be. It's too much pressure that ultimately crumbles the unstable throne upon which you placed the person. You'll be disappointed in the end, and the lesson will be for you more than anyone; you will be to blame for his/ her fall from undeserved, undue glory. Our Boaz is a godsend. If you have one, be so very thankful. If that person in your life is not even remotely akin to the kinsman redeemer Boaz was to Ruth, then for goodness sake, pray! Love! Appreciate what attracted you in the first place. Give to God what you cannot control. Trust Him to give you wisdom in the meantime.

Questions and Reflections:

1. What stood out to you in the scripture reading today?

2. Answer at least one of the pondering questions?

3. Personalize the prayer for your own life below:

DAY 16

Scripture Reading: Hosea 2: 6 - 10

Boaz ordered his men not to touch Ruth. He also ordered she drink water from the vessels his men had drawn. He didn't want Ruth to be harmed, and he wanted her thirst quenched. We don't have to worry about God's protection and provision in our lives. He is not going to allow Satan to take us out from under His love. We may have a full day's work ahead of us. We will have battles, and we will have to fight them. But God loves us, and He knows our eternal souls will be protected. As long as we stay in His field, we have nothing to fear. We do not even have to fear death, for to die in battle is to be ushered into His Divine Presence. Ruth could safely glean in Boaz's fields; we can safely glean in the harvest field of our Lord.

Pondering Thoughts:

When has God sent divine protection for you in your life? How did that protection come? Have you ever experienced a time when you doubted God? How did you realize you could trust Him no matter what?

Praise and Petitions:

The True Vine, thank you for divine protection and provision. I know I can trust you in all things, but help my unbelief. Help me when my faith wavers because of things I cannot see. I ask this in your name, Amen.

Prayer Journaling Notes:

Points from the Editor:

He has done it before hasn't He? Name a time when He placed a hand of protection on you. Now, name another time, and another time. All we need to do is look back when doubt looms. All He ever wants to do is protect us. We, at times, step outside of His protection by our actions, and we fall prey to the consequences. We sure can't blame Him when we get out there on our own limb. Even in our unfaithfulness, He is still faithful (2 Timothy 2:13). Do you believe that? He doesn't expect perfection in exchange for protection. Our Creator took dust to make us. He knows the only way we are even breathing is because of the life He breathed into us. We are living because of the protection He died to give us! He goes before us, and He is our rear guard. He's making sure we have all we need. You can trust Him to do it again and again. Just stay in His field.

Questions and Reflections:

1. What stood out to you in the scripture reading today?

2. Answer at least one of the pondering questions?

3. Personalize the prayer for your own life below:

DAY 17

Scripture Reading: Hosea 2: 11 - 15

Ruth asked Boaz why he is so kind to her in the field. He told her because he has heard of all she had done for Naomi. But he goes further to tell her he knows she is under the wings of God. What a comfort to know! We can take courage in knowing the things we do on this earth do make a difference. There are times when helping Naomi may grow tiresome, but hang on! Boaz is watching! Not only will your work be noticed on this earth, but your Heavenly Father is protecting you and sheltering you under His Wings. So take comfort in what you must do each day, even when the gleaning seems small and insignificant. You are important to others, like Boaz and Naomi, but you are REALLY important to God.

Pondering Thoughts:

When have you felt most useful to God and others? How did it make you feel to know your work was appreciated? What do you do to make sure others know you appreciate their work for the Kingdom? Everyone likes to know he/she is doing a great job, and it really doesn't take a whole lot to give an affirmation.

Praise and Petitions:

The Truth, I praise you because I can always count on your Word. There is no dishonesty found in you. Help me to be the kind of person others notice for your Glory in what is done. I don't want to be a stumbling block. I want to always be found under your wings. I pray this in your name, Amen.

Prayer Journaling Notes:

Points from the Editor:

Be specific. Let the power of life in your words be remembered forever. Say, "You are great." Yes, but say, "You are great because..." "You inspire me because, ..." "You are an encouragement because..." The words we speak have the power to attach to people and help them to truly take on the labels and character traits we believe they already own. In asking an artist recently to donate a painting for our county's library art auction, she replied she wasn't confident in her work. She would really have to pray about it. Wow! I had been watching her on social media, and her work was worthy of her own confidence for sure. I spoke that into her life having never met her face-to-face. I still have not met her, but my words (as a vessel of the Holy Spirit) sprung to life inside of her soul. She did make the donation, and it was a beautiful piece of art!

Questions and Reflections:

1. What stood out to you in the scripture reading today?

2. Answer at least one of the pondering questions?

3. Personalize the prayer for your own life below:

DAY 18

Scripture Reading: Hosea 2: 16 - 23

As Ruth works and grows hungry, she is instructed by Boaz to come eat with his reapers. But he tells her to eat the roasted kernels as well as to dip her bread morsels in the vinegar they have for the reapers. This was a very special gesture on the part of Boaz. The vinegar was used as a refreshing and cooling part of the meal in the field. It is likely had she been left to her own resources, Ruth would have only had access to water. But Boaz made sure she had vinegar. He also made sure she had the roasted kernels, which were the very best of the field. Ruth may not have understood the meaning behind his gestures of kindness, but you can rest assured the rest of the field could tell. When God decides to point you out, you don't have to say or do anything extra. Those around you will know you have an anointing on your life. Be graceful and accept God's gifts to you. Dip your bread in the vinegar and enjoy the blessing!

Pondering Thoughts:

Have you ever just thought about blessing someone for who he/she is? How did you allow this person to stand out? Have you ever been blessed by someone with the finer things in life? How did that make you feel to be singled out? Ruth didn't understand why, but I'm sure she appreciated those kind acts shown to her in the barley field.

Praise and Petitions:

Wonderful, you make all your children feel special. You call us out and send us blessings we do not deserve. Thank you for each time you have sent me a special gift. Help me to bless others as you have blessed me, or at least in some part. I know I can never repay you, but don't let me ever stop trying. I ask this in your name, Amen.

Prayer Journaling Notes:

Points from the Editor:

Recently I had a unique opportunity to attend a special book signing for a well-known author. As I settled into my seat about half way back, I had a sweet lady I don't know really well come up and ask me to join her on the very front. I had recently had a book signing myself at the local library, but this event was huge! I felt so humbled and honored she would think enough of me to reach out the way she did - to pick me out and usher me to an awesome seat. I hope she knows I will never forget it. When you are shown favor, do not gloat. Do not brag. Do not grow prideful. God knows who can handle it and who is not ready for it. It's a test He places before us personally to prove to our own souls that we can accept favor with a graceful response.

Questions and Reflections:

1. What stood out to you in the scripture reading today?

2. Answer at least one of the pondering questions?

3. Personalize the prayer for your own life below:

DAY 19

Scripture Reading: Hosea 3: 1 - 5

Boaz instructed his reapers to allow Ruth to glean, even from the sheaves they had already gathered. He also told them to drop handfuls of purposeful barley for her. He wanted to provide for Ruth and Naomi. He wanted Ruth to know he would protect her and care for her. If you are going to have to work in a barley field all day, it's nice to have a Boaz who is leaving you extra barley along the way. That's how God is with us. While He does require us to work, He makes the load lighter for us. Jesus tells us to come unto Him for His yoke is easy, and His burden is light. Ruth had found her a sweet spot to gather barley. Don't you just love it when you find a sweet spot in this Christian walk where you feel like you accomplish great things for the Lord? I know I do!

Pondering Thoughts:

Think back to a time when you found a sweet spot in your life. What did you accomplish during this time? How long has it been since you had a sweet spot? What would you be willing to do to find one again?

Praise and Petitions:

The Word, you are true and faithful. You always provide bountifully for our lives. Help me to look for where you want me to be and appreciate the good things you give to me each day. I want to find your handfuls of purpose for my life. Lead me to the sheaves of barley for me. I ask this in your name, Amen.

Prayer Journaling Notes:

Points from the Editor:

The sweet spot is the most energizing place for me. It's a place of fruit bearing. When someone else recognizes it as your sweet spot, then it's like a wildfire. It doesn't have to be only in the church or even church work. Everything we do to the glory of God is included as ministry. If God gets the glory for an excellent business strategy, then it's promoting His Kingdom's purpose. We can't just compartmentalize faith and put it in a box inside the church. When excellent character, financial management, business principles, or leadership style is displayed in you, you get a chance to witness of God's faithfulness. It's a platform, and the world around you is watching to see how you'll use it.

Questions and Reflections:

1. What stood out to you in the scripture reading today?

2. Answer at least one of the pondering questions?

3. Personalize the prayer for your own life below:

DAY 20

Scripture Reading: Hosea 4: 1 - 5

Ruth shared with Naomi all that had happened to her in the field of Boaz. Naomi was old enough to know this was not normal gleaning. She knew God was moving in their family. She gave Ruth good advice, perhaps for the first time in their relationship. She knew Ruth needed to stay in the field of Boaz. Ruth listened to her mother-in-law and took her advice. Ruth was not so independent she couldn't take instruction from her mother-in-law. There are times when God blesses us, and we suddenly think we have somehow risen above others. Ruth knew her place, and she remained humble and faithful. Ruth did not lose sight of her purpose in her family. Stay focused and humble in your gleaning in the barley fields. Don't let a few handfuls of purpose steer you in the wrong direction.

Pondering Thoughts:

How do you take instruction from others? Do you find it easy or difficult? When is it easier for you? When do you find it more difficult? How do you approach someone younger as you seek to give her advice? How is it received?

Praise and Petitions:

Consolation of Israel, I thank you for every mother figure you have sent my way in my Christian journey. Help me to always know the value of Godly wisdom from my elders. Help me to provide Godly training for those who are younger than I. I ask this in your name, Amen.

Prayer Journaling Notes:

Points from the Editor:

One of the best things we can do is to take time to listen to the wisdom of those older than we are. Just because someone is older does not mean her/she is automatically wiser. Watch his/her life, and carefully observe outcomes. Then it's okay to not only imitate him/her but to seek wise counsel from him/her. I believe Ruth may have seen Naomi's instruction as confirmation of what she already sensed from the encounters with Boaz's reapers and from the Spirit of God moving her to follow His lead. I can only speculate. But often times matters for which we seek wisdom are already in motion for our good when wisdom comes as confirmation.

Questions and Reflections:

1. What stood out to you in the scripture reading today?

2. Answer at least one of the pondering questions?

3. Personalize the prayer for your own life below:

DAY 21

Scripture Reading: Hosea 4: 6 - 10

Naomi devised a plan for Ruth to gain full access to all Boaz had to offer. She knew the custom, and she knew Boaz. Naomi told Ruth exactly what she had to do and how to do it. I'm quite sure Ruth probably questioned the strange orders, but never-the-less, Ruth got dressed, anointed herself, and went to lay down at the feet of Boaz. Have you ever been told to do something completely strange? It sure makes it difficult to follow through when you don't know what will be. Sometimes God just likes to shake things up for us and make us wonder what in the world is happening. Well, take advice from Ruth. Go clean up. Get dressed up. And show up. Do what God is calling you to do no matter how strange it may sound. God knows what He is doing. Naomi knew; Ruth obeyed! Boaz got himself a bride.

Pondering Thoughts:

What strange thing has God placed on your heart? Did you do it? If so, what happened? What did you learn from the experience? If you have never felt the urge to do something strange, what will you do when it does happen?

Praise and Petitions:

Rabbi, thank you for teaching us in all things. Thank you for showing us the strange things you often require. Help me to be willing to trust you and not question when you do lead me to do things that make me feel uncomfortable. I ask this in your name, Amen.

Prayer Journaling Notes:

Points from the Editor:

It happens to me - God will just give me a video cut in my mind of exactly what I'm to do. I could not plan it better, and many times my mind had not even been creative enough to think it up! I was going to visit a former teacher the next day. She had been in the hospital for quire a few weeks. I was not sure if maybe she would already be released before I could even get to her. We were limited on income, but the night before as I was washing my face and getting ready for bed, I thought of what I could bring with me as a little gift. Instantly God showed me a little snip in my mind of packing a gift bag with everything I would need to give her a pedicure. Really God? I learned now not to even get into reasoning with God. It never works. I did try, but instead I gave in, followed my personal movie clip, and marched right in there. Wouldn't you know it - she was still right there and agreed to receive my gift from God Himself to her! He wants to use us to bless others. Let Him. Even if it is strange!

Questions and Reflections:

1. What stood out to you in the scripture reading today?

2. Answer at least one of the pondering questions?

3. Personalize the prayer for your own life below:

DAY 22

Scripture Reading: Hosea 4: 11 - 15

Sometimes you just have to ask! Ruth laid down at Boaz's feet, and at some point during the night he awakened to discover her. It startled him and caught him off guard, but Ruth figured she might as well ask. Ruth reminded Boaz he was her near kindred, and she needed an heir for her husband's name to stay alive. Wow! Talk about telling him like it was. Boaz, obviously taken aback, blessed her for caring so much about her family. Boaz told her he would see what could be done. Then he told her to rest. God tells us in His word we can come boldly before Him to make our petitions known. Ruth came for the right reason, and she left with a solution. There are times in our lives when we just have to be courageous and ask for what we need. Be a Ruth! Be bold and courageous and bring your petitions before God.

Pondering Thoughts:

Have you ever needed to get a prayer through? Were you able to get an answer? Record a time in your life when you needed God to intervene, and He did just that for you. What happened? How did this event change your life?

Praise and Petitions:

God, who taketh vengeance, thank you for your divine interventions in my life. Help me to be willing to come before you with petitions I need answered in my life. I know you love me and want to help me. I just need the confidence you will hear me and the confidence to ask. I do ask this in your name, Amen.

Prayer Journaling Notes:

Points from the Editor:

It's the fellowship He loves most. Nothing pleases the heart of God more than for His children to engage with Him in conversation. Not always coming with requests, but yes coming with requests. The Bible tells us before a word is on our tongue He knows it, and He knows what we need before we ever ask. So, why? Why do we have to ask? Daddy once told me anytime he heard Momma mention a thing she wanted or wished for he would set his heart and mind on figuring a way to make it happen. Our Father wants so much to give us the desires of our hearts, but He does so as we delight in Him. Ask Him first to become the delight of your heart if that's a step you need to personally take. He's taking care of the rest. He owns everything and can give you anything in accordance with His will for your life He wants to give you. I can promise you this, if it's not His will, you don't want it.

Questions and Reflections:

1. What stood out to you in the scripture reading today?

2. Answer at least one of the pondering questions?

3. Personalize the prayer for your own life below:

DAY 23

Scripture Reading: Hosea 4: 16 - 19

Boaz sends Ruth back to Naomi with six measures of barley. This is significant. First of all, it shows his kindness to Ruth so others would not see her leaving his threshing floor empty handed. To do so might indicate she had been there for "other" reasons. Second, six measures is proof to Naomi that Boaz fully intends to do what he can to make sure Naomi's heritage is preserved. Ruth takes the barley to her mother-in-law, and they both rejoice. Naomi tells Ruth that Boaz will not rest until he has a solution for them. God will not rest until He has a plan for our lives and sees it to fruition. You can rest assured if He has a plan for you, He will make sure you have what you need to get it accomplished.

Pondering Thoughts:

Have you ever walked away from church or a situation in unbelief with how much God just blessed you? How did He bless you? What did you do with the blessing? How hard is it for you to wait for God's timing when you know something good is about to happen?

Praise and Petitions:

Root of David, just as Boaz made a commitment to Ruth, you have promised and made everlasting covenants with your people. Help me to trust those covenants and to patiently wait for them to come to pass. So many times I get in a hurry, and I need you to help me be patient and wait on you. I ask this in your name, Amen.

Prayer Journaling Notes:

Points from the Editor:

If you are thwarting God's plan, He will not rest. If you are unsure of God's plan, He will not rest. If you don't believe God's plan, He will not rest. Our God does not slumber or sleep. He's not taking a nap. He's not on break. He's not slack concerning His promises. He's not more interested in someone else's life. He's not ignoring you. When there is a lull in progress, there is a God-sized reason for it. There's a right time and right place for the solution to replace the problem. He alone picks that time. Your intervention ahead of His timing should be something you'll regret later. When He is ready, you'll be ready too.

Questions and Reflections:

1. What stood out to you in the scripture reading today?

2. Answer at least one of the pondering questions?

3. Personalize the prayer for your own life below:

DAY 24

Scripture Reading: Hosea 5: 1 - 5

Boaz goes to the elders of the city to bargain for Ruth. What a beautiful picture of a redeemer! Ruth, the Moabite girl who many felt was not worth saving, found a redeemer in Israel. She found someone who felt she was worth saving. Boaz challenges the one who had the right over Ruth. Even though Satan had our souls due to the fall of man, Jesus, our Redeemer, challenged him on the cross for our souls. We were not worthy, but Jesus wanted to save our seed, our heritage. We had lost our heritage to death due to our own human actions, but our wonderful Boaz steps up to the gates of the city and declares, "Save them, or allow me to do so." That is truly love.

Pondering Thoughts:

Do you remember when Jesus redeemed you? How did you feel when Jesus called your name out and said, "I want her!" Think back to your conversion and all the emotions you felt from that day. Share them on the pages of your journal. Share them with another Ruth who needs to hear about redemption day.

Praise and Petitions:

God, who is rich in mercy, thank you for redeeming my soul from your enemy, Satan. Thank you for caring enough about me to send your Son. I pray for the salvation of my family, and I long to see the day some of them accept your redemption. I ask for your blessing to see this happen. I ask this in your name, Amen.

Prayer Journaling Notes:

Points from the Editor:

You were worth redeeming. He would have redeemed you if you were the only one. He would have paid the same price for your soul - the price of blood from a perfect spotless Lamb. As a matter-of-a-fact, the auction day was planned before the foundation of the world. He knew you would need a Kinsman Redeemer. He couldn't fathom life without you. As you were presented, bringing nothing to offer really. Maybe used up. Maybe just a child. Maybe poor. Even rich. He didn't need your riches, your beauty, or anything of earthly value. He just loved you beyond measure, so you were bought with a great price. Aren't you glad?

Questions and Reflections:

1. What stood out to you in the scripture reading today?

2. Answer at least one of the pondering questions?

3. Personalize the prayer for your own life below:

DAY 25

Scripture Reading: Hosea 5: 6 - 10

A nearer kinsman had first rights to buy the field of Naomi, and Boaz went to the city to remind the kinsman of his right. But with it would come Ruth and the seed for Naomi's family to live. The kinsmen wanted the field, but he didn't want the responsibility of Ruth. He had not watched her in the barley field. He had not seen her dedication. He only wanted to plunder the field of Naomi's heritage. He didn't want to take the risk with Naomi taking part of his own field with her offspring from Ruth. Boaz didn't care what he had to give; he wanted Ruth. He wanted to save their heritage. He was wealthy enough to take the risk. Satan doesn't care about you or me. He only wants to use what we have, our heritage, to fight his futile battle against God. He wants to use us up and then kill us. But God, our spiritual Boaz, wants to use His wealth and resources to save us. What an awesome Redeemer!

Pondering Thoughts:

How does it make you feel to know God doesn't care what the cost, He just wants you? What a privilege to have such a Redeemer! How can we best serve Him and attempt to repay His great kindness to us? What will you offer Him from the barley fields of your life?

Praise and Petitions:

God, who is blessed forever, thank you for sharing your blessing with me. I did not deserve your redemption, yet you gave it so freely. Help me to show others how important they are to you. Help me to reap bountifully in your great barley field for your Kingdom. I ask this in your name, Amen.

Prayer Journaling Notes:

Points from the Editor:

Boaz had been watching. He had the heart for the woman he had seen in the fields. He had a made up mind. Just like our Kinsman Redeemer, he wanted the treasure of a relationship with the person - even if she came with nothing else. She alone was worth whatever he had to pay. Never forget that. Boaz is just an earthly illustration of heavenly intervention. We see it throughout Scripture, maybe because God knew it would be the only way we could see even a fraction of His plan, His love, and His sovereignty. Maybe God inspired the writers to see it and be endeared to sinful man majestically marked by His image. It's His image in which we were created that brings any good out of us. It's all Him.

Questions and Reflections:

1. What stood out to you in the scripture reading today?

2. Answer at least one of the pondering questions?

3. Personalize the prayer for your own life below:

DAY 26

Scripture Reading: Hosea 5: 11 - 15

The kinsmen took his shoe off and gave it to Boaz. He renounced his right to the field as well as his right to marry Ruth. Boaz was now free to claim both as his own. The kinsmen could no longer claim rights to walk in the field or to take Ruth as his wife. When Satan took his swing at Jesus on the cross, he gave up his shoe. Jesus bombarded Satan's lair and took the keys right out of his hands. Satan no longer has a right to any claim over a child of God. We just need to run to our Redeemer. He paid the pardon, and He has the kinsmen's shoe. We do not have to worry about belonging to someone who doesn't care for us. Our Redeemer longs to have an intimate relationship with us, forever. We are loved. We are protected. We are known in the city as His bride.

Pondering Thoughts:

Don't you love knowing Jesus loves you so much He would proclaim your name not only from the city but the heavens? How does it make you feel to know you are so loved? Earthly relationships may end, but you can be the eternal bride of Christ. What an awesome privilege!

Praise and Petitions:

Thou who my soul loveth, I can never love you in the manner in which you love me daily. But I never want to stop trying. You are my Redeemer, and I love you with all I know how to love you. Help me to discover more ways to show you my love each day. I ask this in your name, Amen.

Prayer Journaling Notes:

Points from the Editor:

He's my husband. I'm not sure men can see Christ quite the same way as women can - even those of us who have husbands on earth. I know God's love for me trumps any earthly love no matter how dear or deep. He is the little girl's treasured true love. The young lady's divine courtship. The unmarried virgin's commitment to purity, and the married woman's Best Friend. He is the widow's Husband. He is the ultimate Lover of my soul. No one deserves that place - that intimate relationship free of all drama. When you know Him like that, you will love Him like that. And He will always, always, always love you back way more.

Questions and Reflections:

1. What stood out to you in the scripture reading today?

2. Answer at least one of the pondering questions?

3. Personalize the prayer for your own life below:

DAY 27

Scripture Reading: Hosea 7: 1 - 5

In front of all the witnesses of the city, Boaz declares his intention to marry Ruth and raise up the dead seed from her husband. He fulfills his promise to give Naomi and Ruth hope. He does so with much honor, and the men of the city bless him and pray for him to have a bountiful seed. Little did they know just how bountiful this seed would be. My heart is overwhelmed with joy as I think about how bountiful the love is for me by my own Redeemer. He shouts my name from the heavens. I am His. He cared not the price for me, but rather He only wanted me to become His. Oh Dear Ruth, do not ever doubt just how much you mean to your Boaz! Never underestimate His love for you!

Pondering Thoughts:

God is jealous for me. He loves like a hurricane, and I am a tree. Bending beneath the weight of His mercy! What would your song be today? How would you pen the thoughts of what God means to you and how deep your love is to Him? Pen the words. Sing them in your heart!

Praise and Petitions:

Thou preserver of men, your love story with mankind is great. You love so deeply I cannot even absorb all of the love you share. Help me to love you deeper. Help me to serve you more. Help me to be the Ruth you want me to be. I ask this in your name, Amen.

Prayer Journaling Notes:

Points from the Editor:

You are enough. You are good enough. You are imperfectly perfect enough. You are Christian enough. You are sinful enough to need redemption. You are treasured enough to be counted as part of the inheritance of the saints. You are saintly enough. Loved enough. Cherished. Forgiven. Accepted. Beloved. Chosen. That's worth the best love letter you could ever pen to the Lover who will never walk out on you.

Questions and Reflections:

1. What stood out to you in the scripture reading today?

2. Answer at least one of the pondering questions?

3. Personalize the prayer for your own life below:

DAY 28

Boaz marries Ruth; she conceives. What! Oh yes! She finally has that little burst of life living inside of her. What a dream! She had been barren for so many years. Mahlon and Ruth likely wanted children, but he was unable to provide her with the desire of her heart. And yet, now, from a man who was an unlikely soulmate, a Hebrew, Boaz has given her a fertile seed. They are with child. Something is changing. Her destiny is looking brighter and brighter. Moab is in the past. The barley fields are in the past. The harvest is gathered. Her redeemer has purchased the right to have her. She is his wife, and now... finally... Her husband's name will live through another.

Pondering Thoughts:

How does it feel to go from sterile to fertile? Have you ever had a dream that just seemed empty, then all of the sudden God caused life to form in it? Think about your dreams. What do you so long for God to do in your life? What has He done to bless you already? Have you experienced the blessings of your Boaz?

Praise and Petitions:

The Invisible God, I praise you for every dream, every prayer, and every time you have come to my rescue. I cannot thank you enough for all you have done for me. Help me to appreciate you more each day. Help me to enjoy the blessings of Boaz. I ask this in your name, Amen.

Prayer Journaling Notes:

Points from the Editor:

Don't give up on your dream. If you have one inside of you, it is like a pregnancy, hope for a life on the outside. God knows. He will give you the desires of your heart as you delight in Him. He's not punishing you if you haven't lived out the dream that is still growing. Even if ever so slowly, if it's a Godly one that you want to sincerely to glorify Him, it's likely He planted it there. Maybe your dream has birthed and already been dashed. God knows. The ultimate dream came true for us as believers is likely eternity with Him. Anything else is only a fraction, and we want to always keep a proper perspective on our dreams. Live in light of eternity. Trust Him with what matters most until then.

Questions and Reflections:

1. What stood out to you in the scripture reading today?

2. Answer at least one of the pondering questions?

3. Personalize the prayer for your own life below:

DAY 29

Scripture Reading: Hosea 7: 11 - 16

Boaz name means "strength." Ruth finally found stability for her life. She found wealth and health. She no longer had to fear dying alone. His name also means "in him there is might." Boaz has such a strong meaning; one of the pillars of the Temple of Solomon was named Boaz. One can only wonder if Solomon thought about his great-great grandfather when this pillar was named. There is one thing for sure and certain, Ruth had no doubt in the strength of her man. He swept into her life from a barley field, and he didn't stop until he gave her the desires of her heart. I can only imagine as she looked back through the pages of her life's journal, to the point in Moab when all she had was mourning, she longed for this day... But I suspect she never dreamt it would be so magnificent.

Pondering Thoughts:

As you look back over your life, what is your own personal testimony? How has God moved for you? If you were to compare Him to Boaz, what are some of the things He's given to you to bring your heritage up from death?

Praise and Petitions:

Rock of my refuge, I cannot thank you enough for all you have done for me. My heart is overwhelmed with love for you. You are such an awesome King. My prayer is that I always serve you faithfully. Please give me the strength to give you all you desire from me. I ask this in your name, Amen.

Prayer Journaling Notes:

Points from the Editor:

It's good to look back with a proper perspective. I bought a book recently entitled "When the Past Won't Let You Go," by H. Norman Wright. I haven't opened its pages yet, but I am very sure the author encourages readers in understanding the past in the proper perspective. Our great Redeemer can and will redeem your past for His glory. We have complete authority to remind God of the past where we saw His hand. If we choose to remind Him of our sins, He won't remember them. We are wasting our time. That you are still drawing breath is a present reality God had His hand in your past. He is right here in your present, and your future in Him and with Him is glorious! Exhale that!

Questions and Reflections:

1. What stood out to you in the scripture reading today?

2. Answer at least one of the pondering questions?

3. Personalize the prayer for your own life below:

DAY 30

Scripture Reading: Hosea 14: 1 - 5

One special day in history, there was a little cry. Little Obed sends out a message to his mother, father, and grandmother. "I'm here!" What a joyous occasion! His name means "a servant who worships." Naomi had a hand in naming him. She has turned from Mara (bitter) back to Naomi, meaning "my delight." God has turned the tide for Naomi. He has richly blessed Boaz and Ruth. They have a son; he will be the father of Jesse. Jesse will be the father of David. What a lineage! What a heritage! A little Moabite woman, all alone in the world except for her bitter mother-in-law becomes the great-grandmother of a mighty King - what a journey! God knew what He was doing in Ruth's life, and He certainly knows what He is doing in our lives. Just hold on! Today you may feel barren, but your Obed is coming! Don't lose faith!

Pondering Thoughts:

Think back to a time in your life when you felt utterly barren of fruit. Now think of a time when you felt God's hand move mightily in your life. Don't you know God loves you? There are reasons for the various seasons in our lives. What did you learn through your barrenness? What did you learn in your fruitfulness? How have you shared your experiences with others?

Praise and Petitions:

The Lamb, I thank you for your sacrifice for me. I praise you for giving to us bountifully even when we don't deserve it. Help me to seek you always and to serve you in barrenness and in plenty. I ask this in your name, Amen.

Prayer Journaling Notes:

Points from the Editor:

Reasons for seasons... If we could just understand that truth. So often we question why we have to endure the twists and turns. We wonder why the state of the good life cannot always be. But, you see, it's the barren and empty places that are producing the fruit bearing. "For our light and momentary troubles are achieving for us an eternal glory that far outweighs them all." 2 Corinthians 4:17 (NIV) You might say, "What I went through was not light!" What Christ went through was not either, but our afflictions are to prepare us for a future all wrapped up in His glory. We may not understand it fully, but we can trust it completely.

Questions and Reflections:

1. What stood out to you in the scripture reading today?

2. Answer at least one of the pondering questions?

3. Personalize the prayer for your own life below:

DAY 31

Scripture Reading: Hosea 14: 6 - 9

The book of Ruth is still read during the Jewish Feast of Pentecost. During this feast, it is believed this is when the Holy Ghost descended upon the disciples and others gathered after Christ's ascension. It is also celebrated by the Jews as a time the harvest of the first fruits has been gathered. The Jews read Ruth to remind them of the importance of the harvest. Christians should be reminded of the redemption price Jesus paid for us, as well as the Spirit He sent to comfort us until He comes again. When you feel like you need to be reminded of redemption, read this beautiful love story one more time. Think about the hope Ruth and Naomi received because of Boaz's sacrifice. But more importantly, think about our own Redeemer, Jesus Christ, and all He promises to those who love Him. Seek to find the greatest qualities of Ruth in your own life. Be worthy of her title. Work and wait on your Redeemer to send you handfuls of purpose in your own life.

Pondering Thoughts:

How did you most identify with Ruth throughout her story? Did you identify with Naomi, and if so, in what ways? What did you learn most from our study, and how will you apply this in your own life?

Praise and Petitions:

Strength to the poor, I am so thankful you care for women like Ruth, for I am a Ruth. Just a Moabite in mourning until you came along to redeem me. I thank you for all you have given me in my life, and I pray I will always live faithful to my Redeemer, my Heavenly Groom. I ask this in your name, Amen.

Prayer Journaling Notes:

Points from the Editor:

Ruth made a commitment to family that surpassed the death of her husband, and provided for her future generations. It's rare today, if not extinct in thought or action to do what Ruth did. But God often asks us to do what is totally unheard of in our culture... forgive those who persecute you. Pray for your enemies. Provide unconditional love to those who least deserve it, to those who should be returning to you that same kind of love. She is our example. God will lead us into Ruth moments in all of our lives for His glory.

Questions and Reflections:

1. What stood out to you in the scripture reading today?

2. Answer at least one of the pondering questions?

3. Personalize the prayer for your own life below:

August
Hannah - The Intercessor

Scripture Reading - Verses about Hannah and her son, Samuel, and Psalm 15

As we launch into the story of Hannah, we should take notice how her battles are slightly different than the other women we have studied the past few months. She has an adversary in the home, the second wife of her husband, but she also battles the scorn and loneliness of being childless. There is no doubt Hannah is loved by her husband, but in her heart, his love was simply not enough. She desperately needed more. So, she went to battle for it. Yet, her battle was won in her prayers. Hannah's prayer to God proved to be more powerful than any sword or other weapon. She did not need a sword once she gained the attention of Almighty God.

Join me as we learn more from Hannah how to use a secret weapon our adversary hates for us to use. The devil knows he cannot be defeated with earthly weapons, but this spiritual weapon cripples his ability to move. Once we have the ear of God, we cannot be defeated. Hannah had learned in quiet anguish of spirit she could connect with the Master of the universe, and He would come to her rescue. Watch what happens when Hannah intercedes for her answer.

DAY 1

Scripture Reading: 1 Samuel 1: 1 - 5

Hannah is a wonderful story of a mother who knew how to intercede. Hannah's Hebrew name consists of three primary letters: cheit (meaning doorway or life); nun (meaning faithfulness); and hei (meaning look or behold). Her name means "gracious" or "favor." It can also be interpreted "God has favored me." From her story we can certainly understand God sent her life. He was faithful to her, and she definitely caught His attention with her prayer. As a result, she was highly favored with the birth of a great prophet as her son, Samuel. I don't know what your biological name may be, but you can definitely become a spiritual Hannah. Do you need something from God? Get His attention! He is faithful, and He will behold you like no other.

Pondering Thoughts:

Think back to a time in your life when you seemed invisible to others around you. How did this invisibility make you feel? How do you seek to gain the attention of God in your life? What are you doing to capture His gaze towards you?

Praise and Petitions:

Chief Cornerstone, I praise you for all you do for me. Thank you for "seeing" me deeply into my inner soul. You know more about me than I know myself. Help me to see others as you would have me see them. Give me favor and help me give others the favor you would have me give. I ask this in your name, Amen.

Prayer Journaling Notes:

Points from the Editor:

God's favor for Hannah would become apparent to her long after He had extended such favor. He knows the children of the once barren when they were barren. He knew the mother He wanted for Samuel. He knew how treasured that longed for son would be to her, what a reward to her faithfulness. Nothing catches the attention of God quite like delighting in Him. Privately, that means cracking open the Word daily, hungering to know Him like you've never known Him before. It means dedicating your life to the fellowship of believers even when they've been less than you had hoped they would be. Less caring. Less loving. Less inclusive. Less accepting. It means giving every single barren day to Him. Trusting Him to work all things for good because you have decided to love Him no matter what. It means looking for ways to serve Him and His people, your family, the less fortunate, and loving those who spitefully use you. He will take notice, and you will be blessed.

Questions and Reflections:

1. What stood out to you in the scripture reading today?

2. Answer at least one of the pondering questions?

3. Personalize the prayer for your own life below:

DAY 2

Scripture Reading: 1 Samuel 1: 6 - 10

Hannah was married to Elkanah, a Levite from Ramathaim Zophim. He was a member of the esteemed Kohathites. Kohathites were part of a special family of the tribe of Levi. They devoted their lives to caring for the Tabernacle and later the Temple. It was their responsibility to move the special objects, such as the Ark, but they had to do so with their own strength. Elkanah's name means "The Lord has possessed." There is every indication Hannah lived in a good home, and yet there was something lacking in her life. Isn't it interesting how we can have so much, yet feel so empty?

Pondering Thoughts:

Have you stopped to count your blessings in life? How blessed are you? In spite of all your blessings, is there something lacking in your life? What would you like to see God provide for you in the future? How are you asking Him to meet the need?

Praise and Petitions:

Deliverer, I thank you for every gift you have given to me. I praise you for all the blessings you so freely give. Help me to always look for those blessings in my life. Provide for me the things I need in order to accomplish your will for my life. I ask this in your name, Amen.

Prayer Journaling Notes:

Points from the Editor:

We've all been there. When we focus on what we lack, we forget the blessings too many to count. It's the secret of contentment - counting blessings. Realizing our very life is held in the hands of the Giver, the Provider, we can rest in knowing the very thing that has captivated us in the moments or seasons of each is that which our God knows is not what we need right then. We may not ever understand why He chose to wait. But suddenly, our lack can turn into one more blessing worth counting for His Glory. I'm waiting for a "suddenly" in His perfect timing. I feel as if I am on the cusp of it; I can almost see it in the distance. But I'm still waiting, and in the wait God is teaching me something new. I just know it.

Questions and Reflections:

1. What stood out to you in the scripture reading today?

2. Answer at least one of the pondering questions?

3. Personalize the prayer for your own life below:

DAY 3

Scripture Reading: 1 Samuel 1: 11 - 15

Hannah was not the only wife of Elkanah; he was also married to Peninnah. She had not just one, but several children. Her name means "jewel;" and the first letter of her Hebrew name is pei (meaning mouth). You can allow your imagination to run wild with this story, but I can visualize Peninnah causing Hannah much distress. It must have been very difficult to have a daily reminder you not only had to share something very sacred, but you had to share it with a boasting, loud know-it-all who thought she was the queen jewel of the kingdom. Yes, those kind existed even in Biblical times. And there are times when God feels they would help us grow in spirit.

Pondering Thoughts:

Have you ever had to deal with a Peninnah? What are some things you learned from your experience? What would be your advice to someone who finds herself in the same place as a "Peninnah?"

Praise and Petitions:

Gracious and Merciful God, I thank you for grace. I know I am not perfect, and I need grace daily, well maybe hourly. Okay, minute-by-minute. Help me to not only receive your grace, but to give grace to others, even the Peninnahs in my life. Help me to have patience and to be hospitable when I don't want to be. I ask this in your name, Amen.

Prayer Journaling Notes:

Points from the Editor:

It's so hard to admit another female is causing much distress. We'd rather pretend we have a handle on it, that the object of our distress is not even worthy of our attention or acknowledgement. But, just today, I was hoping to not get asked a question I did not want to or know how to answer from another dear female in my life. She is dear to me, and I do love her. But her questions often feel like interrogation. And she doesn't understand they are causing me distress; and if I tell her, it may come out mean spirited. It could alter our relationship in the future. In short, don't you be a Peninnah! Don't become the character of the person who brings you distress. She might not mean to. She might already know she does by your silence. She might have already backed off. Just pray!

Questions and Reflections:

1. What stood out to you in the scripture reading today?

2. Answer at least one of the pondering questions?

3. Personalize the prayer for your own life below:

DAY 4

Scripture Reading: 1 Samuel 1: 16 - 20

We are told Peninnah was blessed with children, but Hannah was barren. This was a huge burden for Israelite women. They placed the value of a woman on her ability to bear children in that society. Poor Hannah was heartbroken. Her adversary and greatest rival kept having child after child, and there she was empty. So many times in our lives we see the blessings being poured out on others while we watch from the sidelines of life in depression over our barrenness. Being fruitless is not easy. It's actually painful, yet so many times we feel barren. The world would have us believe we are useless. Hold on. Before you give into those thoughts, remember God loves you. He can turn your sorrow into joy. Today may be Peninnah's day, but tomorrow may be your day.

Pondering Thoughts:

How has barrenness showed up in your life? How did you deal with it? What are some lessons you learned as you walked through your spiritually barren places? How did this strengthen you for the days ahead?

Praise and Petitions:

Immanuel, you are always with us. Thank you for walking with me through the fruitless times in my life. Thank you for showing me there are times when I will feel barren, but it is not a time to quit. Help me move forward and struggle through those times to become productive once again. I ask this in your name, Amen.

Prayer Journaling Notes:

Points from the Editor:

The best lesson of life - you don't really want someone else's blessings. You may think you do, but they are not for you. With someone else's blessings come the attached responsibilities, heartache, and days of suffering. You can't know what they experience, and I can promise you most folks don't blast the downside on social media. Most of us only show the world around us what we are most proud of, or most passionate about in life. You only want the blessings God has for you. And He has promised to strengthen you through the downside of yours He alone knows the blessings we can handle and still praise Him, remember Him. He alone knows the suffering we can handle without it slaying us. We can trust Him for every barren place, every fruitful place.

Questions and Reflections:

1. What stood out to you in the scripture reading today?

2. Answer at least one of the pondering questions?

3. Personalize the prayer for your own life below:

DAY 5

Scripture Reading: 1 Samuel 1: 21 - 25

Elkanah left his mountain of Ephraim at Ramathaim-Zophim (or Ramah) and headed to Shiloh each year. This was a mountainous trek of about 14 miles. It would have been doable, but not an easy task for a man, two wives, and numerous children on foot or burden bearing animals. But Elkanah was faithful to do it. Now Elkanah gave offerings for Peninnah and her children portions to present them before the high priest and his sons (Eli, Hophni, and Phinehas). But unto the Lord for Hannah, Elkanah gave a "worthy portion." You see, he saw her worth in spite of her barrenness. Elkanah really loved Hannah. He wanted to make sure she was blessed. Aren't you glad God loves us in spite of any problems we may have. He blesses us with a "worthy portion." Don't give in to the feelings of inadequacy; God loves you. He really loves you! You are worthy to Him; honorable enough to receive a "worthy portion."

Pondering Thoughts:

Have you ever received a "worthy portion" from God? How did it come? How did you feel when you received it? What makes something a "worthy portion?" How do you distinguish between a portion and a worthy portion?

Praise and Petitions:

King of Glory, thank you for the worthy portions you send my way in life. I know I do not deserve them, but I am thankful for each one. Help me to accept your portions for me and use them to your glory. Help me to also provide others with the portions they need in life as you instruct me. I ask this in your name, Amen.

Prayer Journaling Notes:

Points from the Editor:

Men and women are wired so differently. Sometimes it's so difficult for us to see how or if our spouse really loves us or just tolerates us. But a man often expresses his deep love so differently than a woman. Don't read too many love stories, or at least don't decide that world should be your world. It's a love story - not real life. In a love story there are no real bills to pay, mouths, to feed, tough decisions to make, or loved ones to bury. It's not real, and your life is. Your marriage is real. Treasure it if you have not fallen to the statistics of divorce - it will never be perfect. I saw a quote recently about a perfect marriage consisting of two imperfect people who refuse to give up on each other. The marriage itself is often considered a "worthy portion" for you. Mine is God's gift to me, and I will fight hell itself to treasure the fight God has given me. It's my "worthy portion."

Questions and Reflections:

1. What stood out to you in the scripture reading today?

2. Answer at least one of the pondering questions?

3. Personalize the prayer for your own life below:

DAY 6

Scripture Reading: 1 Samuel 1: 26 - 28

We are told God had shut up Hannah's womb. This is a hard thing for us to understand. This had also happened to Rachel and Sarah. All three women had experienced great grief because of barrenness. There may be times in our lives when God is calling us to suffer barrenness for His divine purpose. No, it doesn't make it any easier knowing it's His will, but at least we have some small comfort in knowing it's not our fault. The barrenness may be for a season, or it could last for a lifetime. And while we may never understand, at least we can trust God. We can take comfort in knowing it is His plan, even if it is not our desire.

Pondering Thoughts:

Do you ever find it difficult excepting God's will? Think back to a time in your own life when you have struggled with a particular direction God was leading you. What did you learn from this experience? What advice would you give to someone who is experiencing barrenness or other difficulties in her walk with the Lord today?

Praise and Petitions:

Jesus Christ, the Righteous, I am thankful you are in control even when I don't understand. I thank you for giving me mercy to walk through the dry places in my life. Help me to understand you will and to walk where you lead me. I ask this in your name, Amen.

Prayer Journaling Notes:

Points from the Editor:

It's the most liberating release of my volitional will - to let go and let God. What other choice do I really have? If you and I really resent we do not have an abundance of options, it will not go well for our spiritual health. But when we open our hands, we release our tightened grip on things we never controlled to begin with. We look up to the heavens, tears filling our desperate eyes, and we wave off the things we cannot control. We surrender our will to be replaced with His will. We are free from the often disastrous results of our own manipulative ways to affect things as if we know best. We don't. We can't think up high enough to match His ways, or His thoughts. Let's pray those very words every day: "Lord, I surrender my will to be replaced with your will again today." For goodness sake, I've been praying if half asleep every morning for years. I still mean it. I just need some sisters to join me!

Questions and Reflections:

1. What stood out to you in the scripture reading today?

2. Answer at least one of the pondering questions?

3. Personalize the prayer for your own life below:

DAY 7

Scripture Reading: 1 Samuel 2: 1 - 5

Peninnah was just a mean girl. She provoked Hannah. She taunted her. Peninnah caused her to worry. She was cruel. Of course, if you lived in a time of polygamy, vying for the affection of your husband, you can only imagine how upset and hurt Hannah must have been. Okay, I'm just going to be honest here. I don't know how she did it. I don't think I could. But yet in our own society, in many ways we women do have situations where we are distraught in our relationships and families. Jealousy is not limited to polygamist families. Watch out for the Peninnahs in your life. They are in your life to steal your joy. They will cause you to fret. But we have to remember we are loved.

Pondering Thoughts:

Do you have a Peninnah in the family, whether physical or spiritual? How has this person stolen your joy? What are you going to do to get it back?

Praise and Petitions:

Majesty on High, I thank you for loving me. I am so glad you are no respecter of persons. Help me remember this when Satan seeks to torment by having me believe you care more for others. Help me to show your love to all I meet. Don't let me ever have the spirit of Peninnah. I ask this in your name, Amen.

Prayer Journaling Notes:

Points from the Editor:

I remember a recent interaction with a friend who had been betrayed by her husband she still deeply loved. I sensed she still wished for him, but when she turned up the song on the radio to an almost deafening level, I knew what I sensed was true. She had a girl crush. The song conveyed the message so clearly; she wanted to taste the lips of the other woman because they would taste like his. She wanted the same blond hair and magic touch. She just knew if she drowned herself in a bottle of the woman's perfume, just maybe the one she still loved would want her as much as she wanted him. Let Peninnah go. You can't control what happened, but many women deal with a Peninnah wanna-be, would-be, or has-been. I don't know about you, but I'm not sharing God's gift to me with another living soul. I will fight for my family - oh, perhaps I've already penned that! We are completely in God's will and way to be jealous for our family - to protect it. It's a covenant before God worth protecting.

Questions and Reflections:

1. What stood out to you in the scripture reading today?

2. Answer at least one of the pondering questions?

3. Personalize the prayer for your own life below:

DAY 8

Scripture Reading: 1 Samuel 2: 6 - 10

In the story, it would seem the provoking of Peninnah was most evident when they went to worship at Shiloh. Perhaps it was because during the rest of the year Hannah did not have to physically see Peninnah or her children. Maybe when they went to worship, Peninnah would show off to all the other women how blessed with children she was. However it happened, we are told during this time, Hannah would become so upset. She would weep, and she would not eat. Sound like depression to you? Oh yes. Hannah was no doubt living a depressed life, and Peninnah certainly did nothing to ease her deepest sorrow. At times we all likely battle depression in one form or another. Look for the signs in your own life. Look for the signs in others. Don't be like Peninnah. Don't glory in another person's pain.

Pondering Thoughts:

How do you battle against depression in your own life? How do you reach out to others who are in a state of depression? How has God helped you overcome the sorrowful times in your life?

Praise and Petitions:

Only Begotten Son of God, thank you for the joy and happiness you give in times of depression and sorrow. Help me always see the brightest times in life and to go through the rough times like a true warrior princess. I ask this in your name, Amen.

Prayer Journaling Notes:

Points from the Editor:

Seasons of depression are somewhat normal and expected - times of loss, not just from death. If we did not love deeply, we would not grieve deeply. But long-term depression, like Hannah likely experienced, is not healthy. She may not have comforted herself or taken steps today's counselors would have encouraged. But you and I can. There is help. I do not presume to understand what that might be for you. I have experienced a season of depression, and I muddled through with weight loss, tears, and other typical symptoms. Thank goodness, it was seasonal, and God totally restored me. Two friends promised they'd never send me their bills. They weren't licensed, but they were priceless treasures to my eventual healing. My God completely carried me. My joy returned. It is a season that marked my life forever, and God is glorified.

Questions and Reflections:

1. What stood out to you in the scripture reading today?

2. Answer at least one of the pondering questions?

3. Personalize the prayer for your own life below:

DAY 9

Scripture Reading: 1 Samuel 2: 11 - 15

Elkanah reached out to Hannah. He didn't like the fact she wept. He couldn't get her to eat. Then he made the fatal mistake of comparing his love to the love of ten sons. I can only imagine in my mind the river of tears and inconsolable crying that must have followed. Don't you just love it when someone tries to give your comfort, and the very things he/she says makes you want to smack him/her? Seriously, did Elkanah really think Hannah wanted to hear those words? There are times in our lives when we just need to be quiet. No words we can say will bring any comfort, and a lot of times they will only incite the depression more for the person. I am reminded of a song I used to hear on the radio, "Quiet please, too much has already been said. Just let it be and learn to listen instead" (Kathleen Harris). So many times we do more harm than good by trying to give counsel when we just need to give an ear.

Pondering Thoughts:

Has someone tried to give you advice? How you feel when it wasn't what you thought you needed? Have you ever struggled to give advice? What advice would you give to someone today who may find himself/herself in the position of Elkanah? What would you say, or not say?

Praise and Petitions:

Redeemer, I thank you for all your counsel. You always know what to say and when to say it. Help me learn the same thing. So many times I open my mouth when I should keep it closed. Help me learn to listen and give comfort. I ask this in your name, Amen.

Prayer Journaling Notes:

Points from the Editor:

It's not your place; It's not my place. Sometimes I am asked for my advice. In those times it is possibly best to walk the asking through options and scenarios. For example, say "If you go this route, the turn out could be this..." or "Have you considered this option yet?" The key is to help the person walk through options he/she can't see. On the flip side, perhaps you are the Hannah in your mind. you cannot be concerned with how terribly Elkanah handled the situation. You can only control your own response. Don't be mean-spirited to an ignorant person. When I say ignorant, I mean he/she doesn't' know all the facts or emotions. You have to make a decision to practice self-control in that moment - to disregard poor judgment. You cannot stoop to that level. It's simply not your place to teach the offensive person a lesson. It will do nothing but stir your anger to nurse the thoughts of how you could respond.

Questions and Reflections:

1. What stood out to you in the scripture reading today?

2. Answer at least one of the pondering questions?

3. Personalize the prayer for your own life below:

DAY 10

Scripture Reading: 1 Samuel 2: 16 - 20

Hannah rose up after they had eaten. Let me emphasis those three words again, **"Hannah rose up!"** Girls, there comes a time in all our lives when we have got to get done with the pity party! There are battles to fight, and there is joy to return. Our continuing to be pitiful discounts (at least in our own minds) what God can do to return joy to us. Yes, we have been hurt. Yes, we have had barrenness. But if we continue to sit around and mope, Peninnah will certainly win. Keep starving yourself in pity, and you won't be fit to help anyone, not even yourself. Notice, it did not say "Elkanah got Hannah up." The Bible says, "Hannah got herself up!" Don't wait for someone to get you up. You recognize the depression for what it is, and then when you are tired of being hungry, make the move. Rise up and go see the King. I know we sing the song, "Take me to the King." But I say for the sake of this message rephrase the song just a little, "Let take me to the King." You are a warrior princess! You can do this. One step at a time is all it takes. Let's rise up!

Pondering Thoughts:

Have you ever just had enough? Enough pining? How did you get up? What caused you to decide to move forward? How can you encourage someone else to take the step? What can you do to rise?

Praise and Petitions:

Strength of Israel, thank you for helping me RISE when it's time to get up! Without your strength I would not be able to do it. But with you, all things are possible. Help me to encourage others to take the first step in rising. I ask this in your name, Amen.

Prayer Journaling Notes:

Points from the Editor:

It feels good for a while; the pity party is deserved. You invite your friends, and because they know where you are, they join you there for a while. You drink from the cup of bitterness, and you offer them some. They agree it tastes horrible; they mourn with you and understand how you must feel. They may even offer very good comfort and advice to you. You may agree, and then they ease out through the same door they first entered. They have to get on with life as they know it. You may even invite more friends. But soon the pity party no longer feels good. You catch a glimpse of your frame in that mirror, and you are thinner or heavier than you were... older... sadder... and life is not what it could be. The party is over, and real life after the pity that used to feel good is so much more what God desires for us.

Questions and Reflections:

1. What stood out to you in the scripture reading today?

2. Answer at least one of the pondering questions?

3. Personalize the prayer for your own life below:

DAY 11

Scripture Reading: 1 Samuel 2: 21 - 25

Hannah finally got down to praying. She had fretted. She had not eaten. She was worried. But finally, Hannah got to the altar. She went to the house of the Lord. Elkanah couldn't do it for her, she had to go for herself. It was battle time. She had lived long enough in the depression and in the humiliation of Peninnah. She was going to war. And when she went to war, she meant business. Hey! Are you tired? Are you ready for a breakthrough? The best place you can find a breakthrough is moving towards the house of the Lord. So many times we hold back. We do not worship when we should. We allow our busy lives or depressed to keep us away from God's house. But when you get serious... When you are ready to see God perform a miracle... You will get up, and you will make your way to the house of the Lord. I don't know about you, but I'm ready! I cannot wait for the word to go forth, "It is time to gather in the house of the Lord." Meet me there!

Pondering Thoughts:

What keeps you from the house of the Lord? Why does it seem in this day we no longer place value on the house of the Lord? Jesus told His followers to sell all and go forward to build the church, yet it seems like in this generation we have devalued its purpose without a reason from Heaven to do so. We need to get back to the house of the Lord!

Praise and Petitions:

Consuming Fire, thank you for meeting me in your house. Help me to build your Kingdom. Consume my life with your presence so I can meet the needs of your people. I ask this in your name, Amen.

Prayer Journaling Notes:

Points from the Editor:

I once heard a comment from a friend undergoing counseling from a terrible divorce. (Aren't they all, though?) Her counselor told her, "When you don't know what to do, keep doing what you know to do." Everything within you wants to cease all daily routines that are part of your functioning life. It takes so much more energy to keep going when depression has stolen the lifeblood out of you. The best thing to do is what Hannah did. She got up. A body in motion stays in motion. A body at rest gets in a mess. We were meant to move, and our energy returns when we do. Don't quit church. Don't quit God. He is for you, and He has established the church for reasons far beyond what we can imagine. If you go for no other apparent reason to yourself, unstrap those bricks on your feet, and go to worship Him.

Questions and Reflections:

1. What stood out to you in the scripture reading today?

2. Answer at least one of the pondering questions?

3. Personalize the prayer for your own life below:

DAY 12

Scripture Reading: 1 Samuel 2: 26 - 30

Hannah made a vow to give her baby back to God. She was so serious she vowed her child to be a Nazarite for life. She promised she would return him to God to serve Him forever. First of all, be warned! Do not vow to God unless you plan on keeping your bargain. God takes vows very seriously. Second, don't promise more than you can deliver. Hannah made this vow to God, and as it turned out, Samuel was able to fulfill his mother's vow. However, be careful. But should you feel so moved, and if you vow, make sure you have every intention of keeping it. There is nothing wrong with entering a covenant with God, but enter it with the utmost intention of keeping it. Don't make foolish vows. Keep the vows you make.

Pondering Thoughts:

Have you ever made a vow to God? What was the vow? How hard has it been to keep it? How do you know when you should vow? What advice would you give to someone who feels like bargaining with God?

Praise and Petitions:

Great Shepherd of the Sheep, I thank you for answering prayers. I thank you for every covenant you have entered with your people. Help me to only vow those things you wish for me to vow, and help me to be faithful as you are to our covenants. Don't let me make foolish vows to you in a desperate move to have your intervention. I ask this in your name, Amen.

Prayer Journaling Notes:

Points from the Editor:

Promises are often empty the moment we make them. It's almost like conviction of the heart when your prayer starts, "Lord if you'll just..." A better starting prayer is "Lord, I want your will. My will is this or that, and I confess that to you. But I surrender my will to you because you know best." One of the best ways to pray in lieu of one more promise is, "Lord, turn my heart to want your will and desire your outcomes above my own." I believe God can turn our desires, and especially when we confess to Him that His are not first. Strap in for the wild ride back to the heart of God minus vows and covenants.

Questions and Reflections:

1. What stood out to you in the scripture reading today?

2. Answer at least one of the pondering questions?

3. Personalize the prayer for your own life below:

DAY 13

Scripture Reading: 1 Samuel 2: 31 - 36

We are told Hannah prayed in her heart. Her lips moved, but her voice was not heard. Yet, we know God heard her. It's not in the noise we make, but rather the sincerity of what we say to God. There are times in our lives when God requires the shouts, and there are times when only a whisper or even a thought is all He needs to know our sincerity. Do not judge others who do not worship like you do. Be careful. Everyone is not moved by God the same. There was absolutely nothing wrong with the way Hannah worshipped. She was meeting God where she was, and He rushed to her to answer her prayer. If you don't feel you have a shout today, don't worry! Whisper to God. He will hear even the faintest call from His children, and He will come running!

Pondering Thoughts:

Do you ever worship God like a whirlwind? How does that make you feel? Are there times when you can only whisper His name? What happens when you simply whisper? Which type of worship best describes you?

Praise and Petitions:

Judge of all the earth, I am thankful you can be found in the whirlwind, in the shouts of victory, in the timbrel and dance, and yet you can still be found in the heart with simply a whisper or a thought. Thank you for always meeting me no matter how I pray or where I pray. I ask you to help me always express my soul to you. I ask this in your name, Amen.

Prayer Journaling Notes:

Points from the Editor:

One night in our children's ministry, a little boy who always prayed out loud for his whole family was sick. He just had a little sniffle, but it changed his demeanor. He was laying around, not really participating. When it came time to pray I tried to pull him in by asking him whether he wanted to come to the circle and pray for his family. He said something I will never forget, "My prayers are all gone." Sometimes we feel that way. Even in those times, God allows His Spirit to intercede for us. "In the same way, the Spirit helps us in our weakness. We do now know what we ought to pray for, but the spirit himself intercedes for us through wordless groans." Romans 8:26 (NIV) But when it's time to shout, my goodness, why hold back!?

Questions and Reflections:

1. What stood out to you in the scripture reading today?

2. Answer at least one of the pondering questions?

3. Personalize the prayer for your own life below:

DAY 14

Scripture Reading: 1 Samuel 3: 1 - 5

Eli, the high priest, mistook Hannah's worship for a drunken stupor. Well, the manner in which she was praying was different. He had likely not seen a woman in the house of the Lord acting like she was acting. So, we will give him a little grace. But a good lesson for us here is to remember just because someone doesn't look or worship just like us is not an indication that person is insincere before God. You don't know what another person is bringing before the Lord. Your struggles may be very different. You may be in a different place in your life. And another perspective to see here is no matter what others may think of you, reach out to God in the manner that moves Him for you. Don't worry Eli may be watching. Find God, and He will help you explain to the Eli in your life. The most important thing is to find God and get His attention.

Pondering Thoughts:

Have you ever judged someone erroneously in the manner in which he/she worshipped? How did you feel when God spoke to you concerning your judgment? Have you ever felt judged? What would you want to say to those who gave judgment against you in your manner of worship?

Praise and Petitions:

My High Tower, shield me from my adversary. Help me to know how to run to you in times of need. Help me to speak the words you want to hear from me. Overshadow me with your wings of protection at all times, even when I can't utter the sorrow of my soul. I ask this in your name, Amen.

Prayer Journaling Notes:

Points from the Editor:

My daughter may never forget a night we were traveling home from church on an alternate route. On that drive home my phone rang, and it was a call I had been praying to receive. My loved one on the other end called to say, "I am a rescue. I believe God has rescued me." It was a breakthrough moment deserving a breakthrough praise that absolutely could not be contained. As soon as I hung up and came to a stop, I completely lost it. I began my uncontrolled, unconfined, uninhibited, and abandoned praise. I did not care she was there. It was really not me, so I cannot defend myself. It was the Spirit of God within me offering a praise, pure and Godly in every way. When I finally got that out from the shut up place in my bones, I looked at my young daughter. She looked at me, and somehow she was not scared half to death. She witnessed pure praise.

Questions and Reflections:

1. What stood out to you in the scripture reading today?

2. Answer at least one of the pondering questions?

3. Personalize the prayer for your own life below:

DAY 15

Scripture Reading: 1 Samuel 3: 6 - 10

Hannah explained to Eli she was not drunk, and she was not a daughter of wickedness (Belial). She explained it was her deep sorrow causing her to act as she did in the house of the Lord. She told Eli, "I have poured out my soul." When was the last time we poured out our souls to God in His house? It is so refreshing to pour out your soul. I'm sure Hannah felt extreme release from the pouring herself to Him. I know I feel release when I simply take it all to Jesus. Pouring out our souls helps us to release all the entanglements of life. It flushes out all the hurt and anguish. As we pour out, we can expect God to pour in healing. I encourage you to make a trip to the house of the Lord and pour out your soul. What a glorious bathing! There's nothing more cleansing than when our souls are purified by God.

Pondering Thoughts:

When was the last time you poured out your soul to God? Why did you need such a cleansing? What had transpired to that point? How did you feel once the cleansing had come to you? How were you able to go back to your situation with a renewal?

Praise and Petitions:

The Eternal God, I praise you for the times of cleansing you allow us to have in your house. I know we must live in Ramah daily, but I am so thankful for the trips to Shiloh. Help me to make more trips to get cleansing as I need it in order to live a productive life for you. I ask this in your name, Amen.

Prayer Journaling Notes:

Points from the Editor:

Not every house of God has quite the same atmosphere of praise, environment for the Spirit of the Lord to roam freely. And the moment you think you've found that place, you might walk in and not feel at home there in the same way everyone else does who shows up every service. It's a conundrum we have to move past to get to the drenching presence of the Lord we so desperately need. I will confess some of my best drenchings do not take place in the house of the Lord. Apologies to all ministry staff and others gathered. It's me. It's not you. I have gushed in my car, on my face, on my knees in my quiet space. What a delight when it happens in church. I could be the open floodgate for others gathered. It could be your move not only drenches you, but moves God and others. What's important is you get what you need from a God who is desperate to meet you there, wherever that is for you.

Questions and Reflections:

1. What stood out to you in the scripture reading today?

2. Answer at least one of the pondering questions?

3. Personalize the prayer for your own life below:

DAY 16

Scripture Reading: 1 Samuel 3: 11 - 15

Eli blessed Hannah. But what I really like is he tells her to "Go in peace!" Remember just a few days ago we saw she arrived depressed, stressed, unwilling to eat. But after her trip to the house of the Lord and Eli's blessing, she is leaving in peace. Isn't it amazing what God will do for us when we allow Him and we pour out to Him? I can only imagine how much lighter Hannah must have felt. Think of the hope that rose in her heart. I wonder if she ate on her way home to Ramah. I would have! After that load had been lifted, I'd have made my way to the nearest steakhouse. Once God answers, it's time to take off the clothes of mourning. It's time to anoint ourselves. It's time to be reminded we are blessed. I can almost imagine Hannah's countenance when she left the house of the Lord. I wonder what Peninnah thought. I imagine the devil running scared.

Pondering Thoughts:

How did you leave the house of the Lord after a prayer was answered? How would you best describe your countenance after that prayer? How would you best describe the reactions of those around you to your new focus on life?

Praise and Petitions:

The True Vine, you move in so many ways. I cannot begin to express how grateful I am you meet all my needs. Thank you for every time you have moved in my behalf. Help me never lose sight of how miraculous you are. I ask this in your name, Amen.

Prayer Journaling Notes:

Points from the Editor:

Peace comes. It eventually comes. We could not survive in our walk of faith very long term without some sense all is well. It often does not show up until we have wrung out our hearts Such a simple truth: No peace, No God. Know peace, Know God. If we ever have come to the saving knowledge of God, His presence was most readily felt and realized because of the peace we experienced after bowing to His gift of salvation. Lot of thieves might try to destroy our peace, but as long as our God who first gave it remains the focus of your heart, your chance at peace is as sure as the winning lottery of all the states, the jackpot of all the casinos. It may feel like your peace has been gambled away by ruthless addicts, but just remember if you had never experienced it yourself you would not understand what you were missing. You would not long for its return. And it can and will return.

Questions and Reflections:

1. What stood out to you in the scripture reading today?

2. Answer at least one of the pondering questions?

3. Personalize the prayer for your own life below:

DAY 17

Scripture Reading: 1 Samuel 3: 16 - 21

Oh, she ate! The Bible says Hannah went on her way, she ate, and she was sad no more. I don't know if she stopped at a Longhorn's on the way. She may have decided it was time for some Mellow Mushroom, or she may have just eaten a bowl of Captain Crunch, but Hannah left the house of the Lord with joy and with an appetite. When God takes your sorrow away, He certainly gives you a hunger. It doesn't take long for the appetite to return after God moves for you. For years Hannah had endured Peninnah and her aggravation, but this year... this trip... this visit to the house of the Lord, Hannah left a different woman. Talk about getting ready to have a baby... Let's go eat! Don't you just love it when God moves in such a way your whole world is set right again! I can't help but think Hannah must have sung all the way to the restaurant!

Pondering Thoughts:

How did you feel when depression or oppression left you? What kind of changes did you experience once you knew you had victory? How would you encourage another warrior princess to wait for the victory?

Praise and Petitions:

The Truth, you are so wonderful. You give us so much hope and such a reason to live in victory. I know there are hard days in our lives, but one day of victory is worth years of sorrow with you. I love you! Help me to always share your joy with others. I ask this in your name, Amen.

Prayer Journaling Notes:

Points from the Editor:

I am personally waiting, like Hannah, for my whole world to be set right again. It's just not all about a baby, thank goodness! When your world is set right, the day is more beautiful, those you love are more precious, and the little things are treasures. And yes, a grilled burger at home tastes like steak from Ruth's Chris Steakhouse. Your thankfulness and gratitude is at peak level. Your love for the God who gave you a second chance is the best testimony to share 24/7. we know what it feels like, we just don't always remember it for the long-term. But let's try. The way to remembrance is always reminders. Keep the scriptures that carried you posted where you can see them. Keep the prayers that wrung you out as constant and daily praises for what God has done. Put some meat on the bones of your frail body and soul. And keep it there.

Questions and Reflections:

1. What stood out to you in the scripture reading today?

2. Answer at least one of the pondering questions?

3. Personalize the prayer for your own life below:

DAY 18

Scripture Reading: 1 Samuel 4: 1 - 5

After Hannah's encounter with Eli, we are told the next morning, Elkanah and Hannah rose up and worshipped the Lord. No, she didn't have a baby yet. She didn't even have a conception yet, but that didn't matter. God had spoken. Eli had blessed her, and she was acting in faith the baby would come. Just because God gives you a blessing doesn't mean the answer arrives right away. There are times you will have to wait for the answer to get to you (like at least nine months for a child to arrive), but you still worship. When God gives you affirmation, you start acting in faith. The pining is over. You rise! You go forward! Hannah had assurance God loved her and would answer the plea of her heart. That was enough for her. It was time to worship! Once God speaks to our hearts, our next actions should be actions of faith He will keep His word.

Pondering Thoughts:

Once God speaks to your heart, what do you do to walk in faith? How do you worship God even when the promise hasn't arrived? What do you say to the barren woman who has received a word but not the promise?

Praise and Petitions:

Wonderful, I know once you speak, I can go to the bank and wait for the cash to show up. You never go back on your word. You always move for your child. I love you, and I praise you for your faithfulness. Help me to never lose sight of your word. I ask this in your name, Amen.

Prayer Journaling Notes:

Points from the Editor:

It's so much easier to wait when we've gotten a confirmation from God the answer is on the way. There are moves you can make, steps you can take when an answer has been confirmed to you. You move ahead in ways you can You speak of, testify of God's faithfulness. You do it by faith. You don't have to tell all the details. As a matter of fact that can really backfire on us if we are not careful. Don't ever presume upon God. Don't gloat. Just tuck that confirmation into your heart, watch and pray. It's just a matter of time. It's just a matter of God's timing, and it is always perfect.

Questions and Reflections:

1. What stood out to you in the scripture reading today?

2. Answer at least one of the pondering questions?

3. Personalize the prayer for your own life below:

DAY 19

Scripture Reading: 1 Samuel 4: 6 - 10

Elkanah and Hannah know each other... God remembers His promise... Hannah conceives her promise... Now even though God had promised, it still took action on Elkanah and Hannah's part. She could have prayed for a child forever, and she would have never had a child unless Elkanah and Hannah performed their act of love for each other in hopes of conceiving their child. If you want God to grow your garden in life, you have got to plant seeds. There's no other way to have a garden. Even in the Eden, the first act God showed Adam and Eve was how to plant a garden. Look at Genesis 2:8 "God planted a garden eastward in Eden." If you want to reap in this life, you have to sow. Elkanah and Hannah had to do their own sowing before the Lord blessed their efforts. Do you want to grow things in your life? Start sowing, then wait for God to bless it.

Pondering Thoughts:

Have you had a time in your life when you needed to take action in order for God to bless your fruit? What happened when you moved? How did God move? What would you tell someone who is waiting for a miracle?

Praise and Petitions:

The Word, I praise you for all the words you give us. I thank you for every promise. Help me to take hold of your promises and to walk in faith while working for you. I ask this in your name, Amen.

Prayer Journaling Notes:

Points from the Editor:

It's hard to know what planting seeds look like, at least spiritually speaking. It's taking actions God ordains for you. It's trusting Him to show you those actions. It's planting God's Word on the inside. It's continuing to pray about your future including the promise of the harvest He has given you. It's small steps really. God is not going to ask you to take uncalculated or radical risks that do not line up with His Word. Talk about getting yourself in trouble! That would do it. Mostly, there is more waiting after the promise has been confirmed. As impatient as we are, God is never in a hurry. If you feel pressured, it's not God. It's likely your enemy who knows His time is short. He constantly uses this anxiety-filled panic or sense of urgency that is senseless and rash. That kind of urgency feeds your fears and removes the instinct of courage and fight inside the child of God.

Questions and Reflections:

1. What stood out to you in the scripture reading today?

2. Answer at least one of the pondering questions?

3. Personalize the prayer for your own life below:

DAY 20

Scripture Reading: 1 Samuel 4: 11 - 15

Hannah's promised child arrives! Samuel is born. She names him Samuel because "she had asked the Lord for him." Samuel's name literally means "heard of God." I cannot imagine her joy. The whole mountain of Ephraim probably heard her singing. As we travel through our own personal journey with the Lord, we will likely all have a special Samuel in life. A time, place, thing, or person that/who comes because God has heard us. It may only happen once in a lifetime, but when it comes, we should rejoice and worship God for such a special gift. The birth of this child validated Hannah's womanhood to her enemy. When God sends us a Samuel, it/he/she also produces a testimony that will live on in our hearts long after Samuel has left home. Hannah likely never forgot what God did for her, and we should not forget His miraculous moves towards us. Rejoice! Samuel is coming! When he comes, sing and dance to the Lord for the miracle! Let the earth know of His goodness!

Pondering Thoughts:

Have you experienced a Samuel in your life? When and how did it happen? How did it change you? How did you respond to others and to God when he/it arrived?

Praise and Petitions:

Consolation of Israel, when you say you have moved, we can count on it. You never fail your people. Help me to always praise you for the Samuel you send in my life. I ask this in your name, Amen.

Prayer Journaling Notes:

Points from the Editor:

I remember praying so hard for my youngest child and only daughter. My faith was still immature enough I was not necessarily praying for His will but mine. I had two healthy boys, and I wanted my healthy baby girl. It was a selfish request really made to what I thought was my personal connection to Divine Destiny. I got my girl, maybe not necessarily because I prayed for her, but because it was God's will anyway. It just worked out that way. But she was planned before the world began. God knew my daughter needed me, and I needed her. He knew she would be the last one in our family to complete us. She's a treasure, and I am thankful God chose me to be her mom just as He chose Hannah to be Samuel's. I think sometimes He answers prayers sometimes out of pure delight.

Questions and Reflections:

1. What stood out to you in the scripture reading today?

2. Answer at least one of the pondering questions?

3. Personalize the prayer for your own life below:

DAY 21

Scripture Reading: 1 Samuel 4: 16 - 22

It came time for Elkanah and the family to go back up to Shiloh, but Hannah did not go this time. She told Elkanah she didn't want to make the trip with Samuel until he is weaned. She knew this will be important, because when she took him, she would leave him to serve in the house of the Lord with Eli. Hannah knew she had made that vow. I know she must have had some reservations about following through with it, but nevertheless, when the time was right, Hannah was going to do what she had promised God she would do. But she didn't rush things. She knew it is important for Samuel to be fully weaned from his mother before she left him. Note in our Western world we think of weaning at about age 2, but in this culture weaning did not mean just weaning from a mother's milk. It likely meant weaning from her guidance and care. It is likely Samuel was about 12 years old when Hannah made that trip to Shiloh to leave him. God doesn't want us to move prematurely. He knows we need to fully grow our seeds before we disperse them. Hold on, and don't rush your Samuel to the house of the Lord. The time will come, and then he will go.

Pondering Thoughts:

Have you ever rushed into something and felt like it just didn't work? What happened? What did you learn from trying to rush God's plans? What advice would you give someone who has a Samuel needing nurturing before releasing?

Praise and Petitions:

Rabbi, help me to realize our Samuels need to be nurtured before we place them into the world. Help me to grow and allow my seeds of faith to grow before I disperse them. I ask this in your name, Amen.

Prayer Journaling Notes:

Points from the Editor:

I have a heart to believe God made her heart stronger for this leg of her journey. The closer she got to weaning day, perhaps the stronger her spirit became when the opposite could have been understandable. To me, when you sincerely make a vow to God in the right attitude of heart, you're set on bringing it to pass in the power of His strength, not yours. A vow to marry is sacredly and sincerely pursued by those who understand the covenant was before God. The hardest part is keeping it when times are difficult. I would think the ceremonial dedication day was perhaps a time that pre-occupied Hannah's heart (and Samuel's). The days and weeks that followed could have been most difficult. But this was God's child. She gave him back with ultimate resolve.

Questions and Reflections:

1. What stood out to you in the scripture reading today?

2. Answer at least one of the pondering questions?

3. Personalize the prayer for your own life below:

DAY 22

Scripture Reading: 1 Samuel 5: 1 - 5

When the time came, Hannah and Elkanah took three bulls, a bottle of wine, and a bushel or more of flour, and they headed to Shiloh. It was time to give Samuel over to the house of the Lord. Notice she didn't take him without anything. She made sure he had food and drink. She made sure her Samuel left home with something to sustain him until she could visit him again. When we give to ministry... when we send out our Samuels... we need to make sure we are putting them in a position to be successful. When God gives us someone to train, we need to impart as much knowledge as we can about the Kingdom. We are called to train, nurture, and then wean our Samuels to go out on their own to do mighty things for God. Samuel was a great prophet, but he had a prophetess for a mother to help him prepare for his ministry in the lives of kings.

Pondering Thoughts:

Who has been placed in your life for you to train? What are you doing to train him/her? Who has been instrumental in your spiritual training? How did he/she give you the training you need to work for the Lord?

Praise and Petitions:

God who taketh vengeance, thank you for your protection. I praise you for the Hannahs and Samuels you have placed in my life. Help me to be the student as well as the teacher you want me to be. I ask this in your name, Amen.

Prayer Journaling Notes:

Points from the Editor:

God gave me that sense of understanding early on, but after all three of my children were in beds under my roof. I was floored with the realization only God knew who those babies would become for His glory. Only He knew what their paths would be. Would their paths be full of twists and turns? Of course they would. Would they be protected from hurt or harm? Would they be saved at a young age? I could not answer all these questions I had, but one thing was clear - it was my place to train them up God's way. No regrets. No looking back. As imperfect parents, we can know we'll make mistakes. We can know, by God's grace, we'll get a few things right. We can and will face our Maker one day with full knowledge He entrusted children to use (spiritual or physical) to raise up and make His name famous. We will have to give an account. I want to be found faithful.

Questions and Reflections:

1. What stood out to you in the scripture reading today?

2. Answer at least one of the pondering questions?

3. Personalize the prayer for your own life below:

DAY 23

Scripture Reading: 1 Samuel 5: 6 - 12

"For this child I prayed..." Yes, those are Hannah's famous words. Hannah reminds Eli years later she was the woman who had been in the house of the Lord praying. She tells him God answered her prayer. Now she has returned to lend. She is giving back. What a powerful woman! What a woman of her word! She didn't have any other children yet. But even though I am quite certain it ripped her heart strings to leave Samuel, she kept her bargain with God. Samuel is released to be the prophet God has called him to be. He will abide in the house of the Lord for his remaining days. He will become a mighty prophet and judge. He would anoint the first and second kings of Israel (Saul and David). I'm sure Hannah had no idea all her son would accomplish, but I am equally sure she knew in her heart it would be great! Oh that we could have the faith of Hannah to release what God gives us! This should be our prayer each day. What a powerful warrior princess of God! Such strength should encourage all of us!

Pondering Thoughts:

Has God ever given you something or someone you felt you had to give back? How did you make the sacrifice? What steps did you take to prepare you heart for the return of that which was lent to you?

Praise and Petitions:

Root of David, you were lent to this earth from your Heavenly Father. You know how it feels to leave your home to help those who cannot help themselves. Help me to be willing to lend and to be lent in this life. I ask this in your name, Amen.

Prayer Journaling Notes:

Points from the Editor:

She had to be a proud Momma though. She had to be proud of Samuel's future - what God would do. I have a heart to believe twelve year old boys were more mature back then. He could have been more ready to face his new responsibility. He likely would have known for years he would be living in the house of God for the rest of his life. He could have been totally submitted to the drills Hannah had used in his years to prepare him the best she could. She had to know the God who answered her prayer was the same God she could trust to place Samuel in His hands. He can be trusted with our Samuels.

Questions and Reflections:

1. What stood out to you in the scripture reading today?

2. Answer at least one of the pondering questions?

3. Personalize the prayer for your own life below:

DAY 24

Scripture Reading: 1 Samuel 6: 1 - 5

Hannah's Song
(part 1)

My heart rejoiceth in the Lord,
mine horn is exalted in the Lord:
my mouth is enlarged over mine enemies;
because I rejoice in thy salvation.
There is none holy as the Lord:
for there is none beside thee:
neither is there any rock like our God.

Hannah writes a beautiful song to God. She shows us we should rejoice in Him. She says her "horn" or "strength" or "flask" is exalted. Her enemies have been brought down! She glories in her salvation. She speaks of God's holiness and His ability to protect her. It is a beautiful song from her heart of what God has done in her life.

Pondering Thoughts:

What are the lyrics of the song of your heart? Write them down. Think about how God has moved in your life. What will your words sing?

Praise and Petitions:

God who is rich in mercy, I could write songs of you until my dying breath. I cannot ever give you enough praise for all you have done. Help me always praise you and never allow the devil to steal my song. I ask this in your name, Amen.

Prayer Journaling Notes:

Points from the Editor:

If we don't have a heart bent to praise, it's easy to forget to do it. We fall to the statistics of 10 healed lepers - only one came back to praise God. But when we do, sisters, we can't help ourselves. Pray to have a rejoicing heart. It's an awesome gift from God allowing joyful laughter at the thought of God's goodness. He allows a complete confidence in the truth of His Word. It allows silent or shouting prayers reminding God of His own faithfulness. Finally, when struggling has ceased, and we are on the other side of a war, battle, or conflict, we can shout victory. When our backs are against the wall, it's all we want. We aren't worried about negotiation, compromise, or concessions. We just want God to show up and show out. He's the King of drama. Just read a few of the true stories in the Holy Scriptures, and you'll see. He loves to display His glory, and you give Him that joy in your struggle.

Questions and Reflections:

1. What stood out to you in the scripture reading today?

2. Answer at least one of the pondering questions?

3. Personalize the prayer for your own life below:

DAY 25

Scripture Reading: 1 Samuel 6: 16 - 10

Hannah's Song
(part 2)

Talk no more so exceeding proudly;
let not arrogancy come out of your mouth:
for the Lord is a God of knowledge,
and by Him actions are weighed...

...so that the barren hath born seven;
and she that hath many children is waxed feeble.
The Lord killeth, and maketh alive:
He bringeth down to the grave, and bringeth up.

Hannah speaks to Peninnah in her song. She tells her to "be quiet," Hannah lets Peninnah know her arrogance has cost Peninnah her health. God has blessed Hannah sevenfold with six children and the love of Elkanah. The Lord has strengthened Hannah and caused her to be blessed. He has given her a song; she is praising Him. There's really no need for us to seek revenge on those who hurt us. God takes care of the enemies of His people. If you feel you have been wronged by someone, pray for that person. Wait for God to take action. His judgment is just. He avenges His people.

Pondering Thoughts:

Why is it so hard to wait for God to move? How do you wait?

Praise and Petitions:

God who is blessed forever, I will pray to wait for you. Amen.

Prayer Journaling Notes:

Points from the Editor:

Mercy does not seek vengeance. It's why the Lord tarries in His return for His children. He wants more on the inside circle of His love, so He waits. Mercy always triumphs over judgment. We may not want the wrath of our enemy, but for wrath to come upon them or to gloat over our enemy's consequences is plain wrong. We do it. We do it often over the same enemies we are called to pray for... to love. It's difficult to remember the whole counsel of God's Word is applicable to the whole of our lives and our responses to negative situations. We humble ourselves to the obedience of the Word when the commands apply to the most difficult places of our lives. The reward comes when our lives glorify the One who sent us into the world to be salt and light.

Questions and Reflections:

1. What stood out to you in the scripture reading today?

2. Answer at least one of the pondering questions?

3. Personalize the prayer for your own life below:

DAY 26

Scripture Reading: 1 Samuel 6: 11 - 15

Hannah's Song
(part 3)

He raiseth up the poor out of the dust,
and lifteth up the beggar from the dunghill,
to set them among princes,
and to make them inherit the throne of glory:
for the pillars of the earth are the Lord's,
and He hath set the world upon them.
He will keep the feet of his saints,
and the wicked shall be silent in darkness;
for by strength shall no man prevail.
The adversaries of the Lord shall be broken to pieces;

Hannah proves to be both poetess and prophetess in her song. She prophesies of a time when Israel will prevail and her enemies will be silenced. She speaks of God's protection for His saints. She writes of destruction for God's enemies. The poem and prophecy have been awakened in Hannah. The world will know her song.

Pondering Thoughts:

Has God given you a word to share with others? What do you feel burning on your heart? How can God use you to help strengthen the church where you worship?

Praise and Petitions:

Thou who my soul loveth, I praise you for the song in my heart. Amen.

Prayer Journaling Notes:

Points from the Editor:

I want our enemies to be silenced. You want the same thing. God promises it will happen. When those who oppose the people of God are silenced, it is proof they have opposed God Himself! I'm like that as a parent, as are most of us. If you mess with my children, you are going to mess with me. Why would we believe God to operate any differently? When He permits Satan to have access to us, He knows the ultimate victory will come as He watches over our persevering faith in the midst of the battle. Then, He knows exactly when it's time to push back the attack of the enemy and make all things right for His child. He is for you, not against you. He will protect you in the midst of battle. He wins in the end.

Questions and Reflections:

1. What stood out to you in the scripture reading today?

2. Answer at least one of the pondering questions?

3. Personalize the prayer for your own life below:

DAY 27

Scripture Reading: 1 Samuel 6: 16 - 21

Each year Elkanah and Hannah made their way to visit Shiloh and see their son, Samuel. Eli blessed them on one occasion after Hannah gave her son a coat she had made him. He told them because Hannah has loaned her son to God, God is going to bless her with more children. After God answers such a prayer like He did for Hannah, I'm sure she didn't expect anything else from Him. But God always gives more than we do. He blessed her with the desires of her heart - more children. When you obey God and loan your talents, time, resources, or even your family back to Him, don't think God doesn't notice your sacrifice. God always gives more. You will never be disappointed for loaning to Him.

Pondering Thoughts:

What is something in your life God has "loaned" or asked to "loan" from you? Have you surrendered, and if so, how difficult was it to give to God? What rewards have you experienced because you gave to God?

Praise and Petitions:

Thou preserver of men, I praise you for all you have given. Help me to give back for all the times you have lent to me. Please show me what you need me to do in order to fulfill your will. I ask this in your name, Amen.

Prayer Journaling Notes:

Points from the Editor:

You cannot out give Him. He cannot help Himself. It's who He is. In both Matthew and Luke, Jesus uses the analogy of a good earthly father to recognize the Giver of all things good, our heavenly Father. "Ask and it will be given to you; seek and you will find; knock and the door will be opened to you. If you, then, though you are evil, know how to give good gifts to your children, how much more will your Father in heaven give good gifts to those who ask Him?" (Matthew 7: 9, 11, NIV) He longs to give His children good gifts. If He's withholding something from you, there's a reason. If a gift comes to you suddenly, it's often because He was waiting (perhaps it's difficult for Him to wait too) until just the right time. He's just as pleased to give as you are to receive.

Questions and Reflections:

1. What stood out to you in the scripture reading today?

2. Answer at least one of the pondering questions?

3. Personalize the prayer for your own life below:

DAY 28

Scripture Reading: 1 Samuel 7: 1 - 5

The scriptures tell us each year Hannah made Samuel a little coat and brought it to him. I can only imagine the love and care she placed into each stitch. It seems to me when Samuel wore his coat, he likely felt the love of his mother embrace him and cover his little body. But more than Hannah's covering, the Lord covered him and protected him. Samuel was living in the house of the Lord, but there were evil men all around him. However Samuel had nothing to fear. He had a mother who made a pact with God a long time before he was born. There is nothing more powerful on earth than a covenant between a warrior princess and her King. Don't ever forget that! If you loan God someone or something, you can rest assured He will take care of him/ her/it!

Pondering Thoughts:

How do you feel when you place the safety of your family into the hands of God? When do you seem to worry more? How does God reassure you He is in control?

Praise and Petitions:

The Invisible God, even when I can't see you, I know you are very near. I know I can trust you. Help me to place the safety of my children into your care and learn to leave them there. I ask this in your name, Amen.

Prayer Journaling Notes:

Points from the Editor:

They are in good hands, the best hands actually. His hands are way more safe than our own. We can only protect our children so much. Bad things will happen to good people. Good things will happen to bad people. In the end, the hands of God are safe. When our children make faulty judgment calls, like we have as children, and as adults, we continue to pray and trust God with their lives. What more can we do? The children are born into this exposed fallen world. This is not heaven, but we can trust the God of heaven to be their Protector on this earth. Release your grip, and hand them over to God. Last time I checked, they were never mine to begin with - just on loan, entrusted to us for a season. Then we blinked.

Questions and Reflections:

1. What stood out to you in the scripture reading today?

2. Answer at least one of the pondering questions?

3. Personalize the prayer for your own life below:

DAY 29

Scripture Reading: 1 Samuel 7: 6 - 10

Hannah and Elkanah lived in the time of judges in Israel. Samuel and his sons would become the last of the judges, and Samuel would anoint Saul as the first king of Israel. Hannah's son brought an end to the leadership of God for Israel. God told Samuel to go ahead and anoint a king. God tells Samuel not to take the rejection of Israel personal. God speaks to him, "They have rejected me, and I will no longer reign over them." In a time when Israel was moving away from God, because of Hannah and Elkanah's faithfulness, Samuel was able to keep the laws of God and please Him. Parenting is so important, and while we cannot control what our children do in life, our Godly influence does not go unnoticed by God.

Pondering Thoughts:

What have your children learned from your Godly training? If you do not have children, what you have personally learned from the Godly training of a parent or other adult in your life?

Praise and Petitions:

Rock of my refuge, thank you for each time you have protected me and my family. I thank you for the Godly training you have sent my way in life. I praise you for my mother, and I pray for the strength to be a Godly influence on my own children/grandchildren. I ask this in your name, Amen.

Prayer Journaling Notes:

Points from the Editor:

Most of the time they don't realize they are training. My parents were living Godly lives, navigating the difficult and blessed days of their marriage. After waiting 12 years without the benefit of fertility treatments, I would suppose their faith was hammered out month-to-month, trusting God with it was most difficult. When we came along, life got complicated, and they kept the faith while four children were nurtured and wide-eyed through it all. Children don't miss much, especially if they are free from many challenges. I would argue even those with challenges absorb much of their childhood like little sponges. We repeated the family lives of our parents before our own three. Unknowingly, we poured our lives in Christ out on them day-after-day. Unsuspecting trainers we were, developing spiritual muscles of our own and subjecting our babies to the mindset we were adopting.

Questions and Reflections:

1. What stood out to you in the scripture reading today?

2. Answer at least one of the pondering questions?

3. Personalize the prayer for your own life below:

DAY 30

Scripture Reading: 1 Samuel 7: 11 - 17

The story of Hannah can be placed in two main acts: (1) Hannah's fear and depression before she turns her circumstances over to God, and (2) Hannah's song and story once she is liberated by the covenant and blessing she received in the house of the Lord. There are defining moments in all our lives. I know I certainly have a few in my life. We all have choices how we allow those defining moments to affect us. Like so many, Hannah fell prey to the crushing impact of depression and anguish because she could not have children. She realized through her prayers only God could take her broken heart and restore her joy. She decided to trust Him, and we see the outcome of her actions towards God. I encourage you to take inventory in your life.

Pondering Thoughts:

What are the defining moments in your life? How would you categorize them: good, bad, etc? When in your life have you ever truly turned something over to God and watched His hand at work? What happened as a result?

Praise and Petitions:

The Lamb, I praise you for every step I have taken in my life. I praise you for every breath you have allowed me to inhale. Please help me live my life to the fullest, and help me realize those moments in time that best define who you want me to be. I ask this in your name, Amen.

Prayer Journaling Notes:

Points from the Editor:

We often fall prey to our own weakness spiritually giving our enemy entrance into our lives only a sovereign God can actually allow. He calls us to strength in Him and total dependence on Him. Daily choices either build or diminish strength for impending difficult times. Difficult times are an absolute reality. Meanwhile be prepared when they come into your life. You have a Savior who has already faced them, and He can walk with you through them. "For we do not have a high priest who is unable to sympathize with our weaknesses, but One who has been tested in every way as we are, yet without sin" (Hebrews 4:15 HCSB). But He will use them to prove you are stronger than you think because you are His child, having obeyed Him in the disciplines of your faith to gain spiritual muscle for the journey. Don't wait for the hard times. Do it now.

Questions and Reflections:

1. What stood out to you in the scripture reading today?

2. Answer at least one of the pondering questions?

3. Personalize the prayer for your own life below:

DAY 31

Scripture Reading: Psalm 15: 1 - 5

Hannah may have lived in a special time in history. She may have had some circumstances in her life unfamiliar to us, like living in a polygamist family. But Hannah's emotions, her struggles, and her victories are not unlike ours at all. If you begin to battle thoughts of depression, think of Hannah. If there is something in your life you want more than anything in the world, but it seems unattainable, think of Hannah. If you are asked to give back to God what you have been given, think of Hannah. One consistency is in spite of all she faced, she never quit going to the house of the Lord. It was there she expressed her deepest anguish of soul; and it was in the house of the Lord she was given her greatest blessings. Learn from her life. Leave the pages of her story more determined to become a greater warrior princess of God.

Pondering Thoughts:

What have you learned from Hannah's story? Where did you most identify with her? What will you take away from going through her life?

Praise and Petitions:

Strength to the Poor, I stand truly amazed when I see your hand move in the lives of your people. Hannah's story has been such an inspiration for me. I pray you help me live my life so my story will encourage those who know me, and perhaps even those who do not. I ask this in your name, Amen.

Prayer Journaling Notes

Points from the Editor:

The house of the Lord was her place of sacrifice. It's where she found love and where she left love. She found the One who is love there. Her love for Him sparked her desire to give her first child back to Him right there in the house of God. There's no place I'd rather be. Sometimes the house of the Lord is a place where hurt was real, acceptance was half-hearted, or prayers were seemingly unanswered. No matter what our feeble minds perceive about the house of God, we can know for sure - it's a place sanctioned by God, inhabited by His Holy Spirit, and wed by Christ Himself - the Bridegroom. You can't hate church and love her Groom. It's impossible. It's where the human relationships are hammered out. It's a safer place than any worldly institution because it's God's. It may feel differently to you, but find a church where you can worship. Be there. Do not forsake the fellowship God initiated and ordained.

Questions and Reflections:

1. What stood out to you in the scripture reading today?

2. Answer at least one of the pondering questions?

3. Personalize the prayer for your own life below:

Final Thoughts

In the past four months, we have gazed into the lives of four very independent, colorful, and gifted warrior princesses (Rahab, Miriam, Ruth, and Hannah). Each of these women had much to share with us. Their lives were in a different time, but so many of their struggles are contemporary to our lives today. It is my prayer the words on these pages have jumped out to you and helped you in your own journey as a warrior princess.

In the final book of this series, we will look at four women who find themselves in New Testament history during and after the time of Christ. We will explore the expeditions of Mary (Jesus' mother), Priscilla, Lois, and Lydia. We will look at their customs, their daily events, and their relationships with our Savior.

Are you ready to embrace your position in history as a warrior princess? I hope you are. I would love to hear your stories and your thoughts as you make this spiritual journey with us. Please email me at sbodom@gmail.com with your thoughts and stories. You can also see our updates on our Warrior Princess of God FaceBook page at: www.facebook.com/warriorprincess2017.

Until next time...

God Bless!

About the Author

Dr. Odom is a woman who is passionate about her family, her church, her profession, and most importantly her King of Kings! She spends most days working in her student and educator motivational company, but when she closes the books each day, she is ready for family. She loves her grandson, Clemens, and spends much time with him. She and Clemens have written several children's books and plan to do even more as he grows. In addition to spending time with her family, Dr. Odom is also a pastor's wife, and she loves her church. She seeks to build Kingdom leaders, especially with her women's ministry. It has been a life-long goal for her to write a women's devotional, and while she never envisioned a 3-book series, the time has finally arrived for her to complete the task.

Dr. Odom can be reached at sbodom@gmail.com. She would love to answer questions about the book, visit other women's ministries, or simply lend a listening ear to someone in need.

You can find all of Dr. Odom's books on Amazon.com by searching for her name, Sarah B. Odom. Her goal is to inspire others as she has been inspired.

About the Contributing Editor

When I asked Mel Ann to edit this series, it was sort of like a favor-for-favor deal. She needed an editor; I needed an editor. Soon I realized she was really "into" editing the series and writing her thoughts at a much deeper level than I had anticipated or had seen with other editors. I decided I wanted to add her thoughts as a reader, to guide others who read it to a deeper experience. Allow me the pleasure to introduce to you my editor and friend, Mel Ann Sullivan.

Mel Ann and her husband live in Millry, Alabama. They have three wonderful children who have entered into the adult phase of their lives. They are serving members of Calvary Baptist Church in Waynesboro, Mississippi, and enjoy simple rural living. Mel Ann holds a B.A. from the School of Communication at the University of Alabama, and loves writing and speaking, both in Christian service and professionally. She has spent most of her career in community banking as a marketing/communications, and community development. She has recently published her first book and e-book entitled *I Need a Better Friend.* You can find the book listed on Amazon.com by searching by book title or author's name.

Coming Soon!

Book 3

Sep: Mary - The Mother
Oct: Priscilla - The Minister
Nov: Lois - The Teacher
Dec: Lydia - The Financier

Published

Book 1

Jan: Deborah - The General
Feb: Jael - The Protector
Mar: Esther - The Mediator
Apr: Abigail - The Advocate

Made in the USA
Lexington, KY
05 September 2017